W9-DHO-202

The GREAT DEPRESSION

and

A Teenager's Fight to Survive

(A Runaway Youth's Adventures in the Great Depression)

by

DUVAL A. EDWARDS

Copyright ©1992 by Duval A. Edwards
Seattle, Washington
All rights reserved, including the right of reproduction in
whole or in part in any form.

FIRST EDITION

RED APPLE PUBLISHING
P. O. Box 101
Gig Harbor, WA 98335

Printed by Gorham Printing
Rochester, Washington

ISBN: 1-880222-07-8

Library of Congress Catalog Card Number: 92-080456

To the memory of

WILLIAM A. and ANN W. OWENS

ACKNOWLEDGMENTS

I am deeply indebted to many friends and family members. Especially helpful were my brother Carl and sisters Oletta and Lela Mae, and friends from my early years in Louisiana and San Antonio who searched their memories to correct errors and omissions on my part.

My sincerest appreciation to old friends Bill and Ann Owens. Bill reviewed the initial draft, provided constructive suggestions and was enthusiastically supportive. His wife, Ann, after Bill's death, did yeoman service in closely editing later revisions until her own recent death.

Special thanks go to Phyllis Hatfield and Elizabeth Wales, both of Seattle, for their professional input, and to my wife, Kay, for her patience and tolerance. Others whose encouraging words served to keep me on course were James Pylant and Davin Bowen, both of Texas, Patricia Van Der Leun (Connecticut and New York), and Christine K. Tomasino of New York City.

DAE

FOREWORD

Duval and I came from the wrong side of the river. We spent our childhood in Pineville, a small town on Red River in central Louisiana populated mostly by proper, but poor, working class families. On the other side of the river, however, was Alexandria, an old river town with grand traditions, where many people lived in elegant houses with lots of servants and drove flashy cars.

In the thirties there was only one high school, Bolton High, for the two towns. Naturally it was located in Alexandria, and Pineville kids were bussed to it in the most awful, tinny vehicles ever devised by man. If we didn't already have an inferiority complex because we lived on the poor side of the river, this bus ride would have given it to us.

The important posts at Bolton, the big athletes, the cheer leaders and members of the private clubs were taken over by children of the establishment families. There was little left for the Pineville kids but to go to classes.

However, Duval was an exception. He was bright, made good grades and wrote the best term themes of anyone in the class. Therefore it was fitting that at the end of his junior year he was elected next year's editor of *Cumtux*, the school's prize-winning newspaper. This was the highest honor awarded to someone from Pineville in recent memory.

Sadly, the following summer that part of Louisiana hit the very bottom of the Great Depression. Duval's father had been unemployed for a long time, and there were many meals when there was not enough food on the table to ward off real hunger. When Duval realized his family could not afford to send him to high school for his final year, he was determined to leave home in search of a job.

So he slipped away and began the great adventure of his life, as told simply in this vivid description of his first six months' battle with the Great Depression. I recommend the book as a refresher course for those who lived through those days, and as an eye-opener for younger generations.

Don Delos Gayer, Librarian
Vizcaya Art Museum, Miami, Florida

TABLE OF CONTENTS

INTRODUCTION

My father was a native Texan and a real working cowboy; he'll always be a "longhorn" to me. As his half-Texan son, does that make me a "shorthorn"? This may have been the subconscious pull that pointed me toward Texas that September morning in 1932 when I personally locked horns with the Great Depression. At age sixteen, I was running away from home in Central Louisiana with a half-year to go to finish high school. After all these years, why would I want to tell the story of this fight to survive the worst months of the modern world's Great Depression?

In 1968, Scott Foresman and Company published a book by Thomas C. Cochran of the University of Pennsylvania titled *The Great Depression and World War II*. It came into my possession a few years ago while I was adding books on World War II to my military library. A number of statements in this small book intrigued me, a child of the Great Depression. It interested me to note the connection Cochran found between the Great Depression and World War II, though he was far from original in this analysis. Memories began to flow.

Then as I began to research and write genealogical items about my family, again digging into the Great Depression years, it gradually dawned on me that I didn't find a single first-hand account of the conditions a runaway teenager faced in the Great Depression.

There have been books of pure fiction and tomes of dry statistics about our Great Depression (see Bibliography). A Canadian book by Pierre Berton entitled *The Great Depression: 1929-1939* published by McClelland & Stewart, Inc. in 1990, is one of the latest. But I know of no written eye-witness account of what it was like for a runaway boy in the U. S. to work, play, dream and just survive growing up in those challenging times.

William A. Owens, a native Texan, and I became good friends during World War II, as Special Agents in the Army's Counter Intelligence Corps [CIC]. A year before Bill's fatal disease first appeared, we began exchanging tales

8

of our teenage years (he has vividly described his experiences in *This Stubborn Soil*). When I told him about boxing Kid Onionhead in Bossier City for a free meal, he exclaimed, "Write it up! Write it up!"

Bill's exhortation was the clincher. I began writing this factual account of my first six months as a runaway youth in 1932 and managed to get a rough draft to Bill for review just as he was entering the twilight zone of his terminal illness. His wife, Ann, continued to encourage and edit my efforts, throughout his illness, and on beyond.

In a sense, this book is a letter directed to people of my generation and younger who survived the Great Depression, and to those who have never had to endure the cold, hunger and hopelessness of the homeless. It is especially intended for the many who are unaware or have forgotten that certain things we take for granted today did not exist in those times: such as, a guaranteed minimum wage, social security, health insurance, unemployment and retirement benefits, insured bank deposits, along with more charities and other local, state and federal government aid.

But it is not the first letter I ever wrote to call attention to something I deeply felt was wrong. In 1928 when I was thirteen and in the sixth grade, Huey P. Long was in the middle of his campaign for governor of Louisiana, bringing his magnetism to every parish and town he could cover. He made it to Pineville where I went to school.

His fiery, patriotic speech in our school kept me mesmerized for days, as it also seemed to affect our parents who attended and voted. Then I awoke from my trance and recalled that our state flag had not been displayed on the stage. I immediately wrote Candidate Long to complain about the absence of this patriotic symbol from my school auditorium. His reply promised the flag would be there on his next visit, especially if I would assist in seeing to it. To my knowledge, Huey never returned.

I do not consider my story especially unique. Millions can recall similar experiences when a tide of homeless people of all ages — including numerous young runaways — flooded the byways of America in 1932 and 1933, the very bottom of the Great Depression. The shame is that our streets

9

are today still crowded with youthful runaways amidst the homeless, though not always for the same reasons as those the Great Depression brought on.

I do not advocate that anyone, young or old, in good times or bad, choose to run away from their home and their problems as I did as a teenager in 1932. Far from it!

But what is so often overlooked is that teenage is a critical period of increased awareness of the real world, when a youngster's consciousness is most vulnerable to stress and pull from many forces — not all of them benign.

For that reason, I urge more open channels of communication between family members, and especially the inclusion of teenagers in family-crisis conferences where they can feel and be a part of the family's problem solving and decision making. If this had been possible in my day, in my family, I would probably have made a different — and better—choice.

"There's a heap o' ways to make a living."
—**William A. Owens**

Chapter 1

GOLDEN GLOVE

The murmur of the crowd intensified as the gym continued to fill. Cigarette and cigar smoke drifted across the fight ring. I looked around for a face I might recognize. No one. Of course, I didn't expect anybody. After all, I was in a town I had never visited before and two days earlier had never suspected I'd be in. Don't look at the crowd, I told myself. Forget it. Just concentrate on what you're supposed to do.

What I was supposed to do was to conquer my opponent in a preliminary bout of the Golden Glove boxing tournament. In this early September of 1932, boxing was very popular in Louisiana in spite of the economic havoc the Great Depression continued to wreak. The famous Sharkey-Schmeling world heavyweight boxing championship had been broadcast over national radio on June 21. I had vivid memories of an earlier, famous Tunney-Dempsey fight. These national events went far toward whetting the appetite of local fans for more.

The Golden Glove tournament for amateurs complemented the program for young boxers then standard in

11

many high schools in the state, which produced interschool tournaments and state championships. But Golden Glove was big-league stuff, not a part of any school system. Its goal was the eventual naming of a national champion in each of several weight divisions specially designed for youths.

Entry into the ring by my flyweight (under 112 pounds) opponent, Kid Onionhead of Shreveport, halted my ruminations. As he took his stool in the opposite corner, for the first time a shiver went up and down my spine, a foreboding of dire things to come.

A flyweight my oddly named adversary may have been, but he was TALLLL! I mentally calculated that his stringbean frame would tower over me by at least a foot. I had weighed in at 108 pounds. He was a couple of pounds heavier, but his arms were clearly several inches longer than mine.

What have I gotten myself into, I thought uneasily.

At that moment I recalled the many occasions on which my father had preached to me and my brothers that "prizefighting," as he called it, was a terrible thing. He even frowned on discussions of our trying out for the popular high school boxing teams.

Yet here I was, in Bossier City, in the northwest corner of Louisiana, just moments away from starting my first match in the Golden Glove prelims — in fact, my first time ever in a boxing ring. Well, I figured, I had rebelled against parental authority when I ran away from home only two days earlier, so going one step more and disobeying a parental injunction never to put on boxing gloves was just a logical next step in that rebellion.

My thoughts were interrupted as the referee motioned Kid Onionhead and me to the center of the ring.

"In this preliminary flyweight bout, we have Kid Duval from Tioga" and he held up my right hand, "going against Kid Onionhead of Shreveport" holding up my opponent's left hand.

The roar of the crowd seemed to favor the local boy, Kid Onionhead, as the city of Shreveport was just across Red River from Bossier City, whereas tiny Tioga where I hailed from, over a hundred miles southeast, was probably unknown and had no appeal to most of the spectators.

In the center of the ring, finally face to face with my

12

fellow gladiator, my shivering increased. As I stared up into his unsmiling face, at least a foot higher than mine, his long, bony arms now looked to be half again the length of mine. How in the world could my gloves penetrate the protective shield his longer reach should give him, I asked myself — and found no immediate answer.

To the applause of a now thoroughly noisy crowd, we returned to our respective corners. As I waited for the starting bell, my mind raced wildly with all kinds of doubts and notions. Out of this chaotic mental jumble there suddenly came a glimmer of a plan: I remembered reading about the famous Dempsey-Tunney world championship fight, in which Tunney mounted his "bicycle" and backpedaled beyond the reach of the legendary awesome fists of Jack Dempsey. It certainly had not hurt Tunney's success. This stratagem had enabled him to actually defeat Dempsey.

My mentor and sponsor had not mentioned this aspect of boxing, but now it lurked at the fringes of my thoughts as the bell rang for round one.

Half pushed by my sponsor who stood just behind me, half impelled by my own efforts, I found myself in the middle of the ring before Onionhead. I stood with my arms held in the guard position, not knowing what awaited me and dreading the unknown.

My rapid entrance into the middle seemed to intimidate Onionhead, for he approached more cautiously. For a long minute we circled each other, feinting with our lefts but neither landing nor trying to land any telling blows, while the crowd noise increased to a roar. The spectators were demanding some real action for their money.

Tentatively, Onionhead began to pepper me with his left fist, holding his threatening right in reserve. Fearing the worst, it was then that I put the Tunney bicycle plan into execution, backing slowly as my opponent advanced with growing confidence. He now seemed to sense my unease, for he accelerated his movements, became more aggressive as he jabbed harder with his leading left, followed up more and more with his right, trying to connect with my chin.

It became increasingly difficult to ward off his blows. And in the final minute of this first of the three rounds allowed in Golden Glove competition he discovered my face. It was obvious that my bicycle did not have the speed of

13

Tunney's!

Left jabs and right swings plastered my jaws, my lips, my nose, my eyes — there seemed to be no letup, no escape from Onionhead's pummelling. Desperately I tried to protect myself, but his long right arm consistently reached over my protection zone. When the clang of the bell signaled the end of round one, I knew I was in for a very sore evening.

My sponsor did not let on that he was disturbed. As he wiped my forehead and rubbed my arms, he said in a low whisper that I had probably lost round one on points, but not to worry — there were two rounds left.

"Get inside and under the Kid's arms," he said.

I didn't have time to explore how I was to accomplish that feat, because just then the bell clanged for round two.

This time I managed to get to the center of the ring on my own, but I did not feel nearly as lively as before. My shivering had stopped and been replaced by a paralyzing numbness. This set my facial muscles into cement and gave me a fixed expression that must have momentarily startled Kid Onionhead, for he did not immediately take up where he had left off in round one.

We circled each other more warily this time. But the crowd continued to clamor for blood, and we finally obliged them. We engaged in a flurry of exchanges and then, to my utter amazement, Onionhead committed the error that ended his Golden Glove hopes — for 1932 anyhow. He surrounded me with his long arms and towering height. And while we were in this clinch, he whispered faintly but clearly in my ear: "Let's take it easy, and neither one of us will be hurt."

Never will I forget those words. They startled me. My opponent could not have picked a better way to get my "fighting Irish" up. Though I had disobeyed my father's injunction against prizefighting, that didn't mean I was ready to throw my entire upbringing out the window. For Dad had taught my siblings and me one very important principle in life: Don't cheat!

And here this overtowering hulk wanted me to cheat this audience of hardworking people, each of whom had paid a hard-earned admission charge to see some real, honest boxing. I literally saw red. Real specks of blood floated in the haze in front of me. Mine, I knew. But the very

14

idea of participating in a fraud made my brain see red, too.

My rage translated into instant action. To Onionhead's astonishment — and obviously to the crowd's as well — I went into double and triple overtime. Pumping both arms, I tore like a windmill into and through Onionhead's defense, bombarding his body and his face with blow after rapid blow so that he reeled backwards — taking his turn on an involuntary, slower Tunney-cycle.

The ferocity and suddenness of my attack took him so by surprise it was all he could do the rest of that round to try to cover his chin, eyes, nose and cheeks with both hands. I wasn't ringsmart enough to know that I should then go for the body, and, besides, I was still under the spell of my indignation — impelled by anger, not reason or a plan.

When the bell ended round two, my sponsor did not have to tell me this had been my round. "Keep it up!" he said as he finished wiping the sweat, mixed with blood, from my cut lip.

The final round began. I was still pumped up with enough adrenaline to beat my opponent to the center of the ring. From the moment I had begun my windmill attack, the crowd had loudly applauded the action. They had deserted their local boy and were now in my corner. The audience yelled for more of the same in this round. The fact that I was much smaller no doubt made me the underdog, and the world seems to love the underdog who has an outside chance of winning.

Kid Onionhead had recovered somewhat from my onslaught and gave me a fairly good fight in round three. But I had just enough indignation-fired muscles left to keep up the momentum. My sponsor told me later that the judges awarded me the victory solely on the last two rounds. Of course! It certainly didn't include the first.

I had won my first boxing match, but I did not feel like a winner. Never had I imagined that a victor could be as bruised, battered and bloody as I was at that moment.

After a hot shower that removed the blood and sweat, but not the hurt, I went with my coach to collect my big prize.

It was against the rules of Golden Glove to award money, so the local sponsors of this preliminary event had decided to treat all contestants, losers and winners alike, to a steak dinner. Getting this free meal had been the main motivation for my entering the contest in the first place.

I'm fairly certain the steak was a good, tender one, but I will never know for sure. Every muscle and bone in my face was so sore that each bite I took brought forth a shot of pain. Each time I chewed I ached; each swallow of milk hurt going down my throat.

Is victory — and a free meal — worth this anguish, I asked myself?

But knowing a motor needs fuel to keep functioning, I ate it all, every painful scrap on my plate. Homeless, jobless, broke, and in a strange city during the depths of the Great Depression, I had no idea when I would eat like this again. But joy I had anticipated in the victory was missing, although the apple pie and ice cream made the meal and the event somewhat more palatable.

While I was trying to do full justice to the dessert, my sponsor sat down beside me, put his hand in a fatherly way on my shoulder (ouch!) and said, "Kid Onionhead has asked for a rematch one week from now. It will have no official bearing in the contests, but he still thinks he can beat you. It's your decision to make. What do you say?"

What can a "champion" say? I had survived my one and only boxing bout. Could I do it again? With the same adversary? For another free meal, anyhow, I thought. So confidently I mumbled, "Sure. Why not?"

"Breakdown of respect for parents and of family sustenance, hope and security, had a serious impact on children brought up between 1929 and 1940."

—Thomas C. Cochran

Chapter 2

HEART OF LOUISIANA

What does a sixteen-year-old amateur boxer do between fights? Especially before a grudge match? No question what to do in my case: find a job.

In the first days of September 1932, instead of enrolling for my final semester as a senior in Bolton High School, Alexandria, Louisiana, I had headed northwest out of Tioga, a small community northeast of Alexandria and Pineville, two cities in the middle of the state. I was running away from home.

With only months to go before I would graduate from high school, why did I pull out and run away? The reason for the decision to do so was extremely complicated, but there are two words that express it concisely: Great Depression. And, at age sixteen, I was headed right into the middle of it.

The Great Depression? What did it mean, what was it all about, why was it so "great"?

Three years before the fight, in October 1929, there was a drastic plunge in the value of stocks on Wall Street in New York City that sent shock waves throughout the world. Ripples from these waves did not reach Louisiana right

17

away, so our small-town family of seven — along with most of our neighbors — became aware of them only gradually.

When this 1929 debacle of the Great Depression began, my father owned and operated an abattoir — a word of French origin well understood in Louisiana, meaning a slaughterhouse where cattle and hogs were butchered. It was located on Holloway-Prairie Road, outside of Pineville, a small town on the east side of Red River, opposite Alexandria, a larger city known as the "Heart of Louisiana."

Our home was situated on a corner of several acres on which cattle grazed and hogs rooted through underbrush while awaiting their turn in the abattoir. The slaughterhouse was at the back part of the acreage.

There Dad had built a successful, small enterprise (with employee Jake Barrett, and a little help from my brothers and me), competing favorably with long-established, independent, local meat producers as well as giant national ones. He supplied beef and pork for many butcher shops and meat markets in Rapides and other central Louisiana parishes.

Unfortunately, Dad trusted people too much. He extended credit time and time again to small retailers who were barely eking out a marginal existence as the Great Depression made inroads on their markets. But his creditors were not as kind to him; they could not wait interminably for their money. Besides, they had lawyers who would sue him, and Dad didn't know how, and had no wish, to go about doing the same to his debtors, whom he considered his friends.

Thus, gradually, as the economy continued to worsen, his abattoir's revenues went down while bill collectors became more insistent. Within a year of the big crash, the inevitable day came. Dad was forced to close his operation. He could fight the battle no more.

We were lucky, however, in that Sim B. Whatley, who managed the Rapides Packing Company, a local independent competitor, had become a good friend of Dad's, admired his cattle savvy, and fully understood the situation. Not only did he arrange for Dad to begin working for Rapides Packing, but he actually made a deal with him to swap our house, plant and acreage for his home at Ball and Singer Streets in Pineville.

18

This exchange of assets did not produce enough revenue to satisfy any but the most urgent of our creditors, and our new home still had a balance on a mortgage, which, of course, it was now Dad's obligation to pay off. But I have always considered it a mark of Dad's good reputation that his former competitor would make such a deal.

When the family moved into its new home in Pineville, and Dad went to work as a cattle buyer for his former chief competitor, Mother acquired an amazing mechanical device called a Maytag washing machine. No longer did she have to use the old washboard and tub as she had all her life; the washing was now done automatically, although there was a wringer attachment that still required elbow grease to get the job finished. We kids often supplied this elbow grease when we weren't at school or working.

With this modern equipment in place, and despite Dad's initial objections, Mother began to do laundry for friends and neighbors for a small fee that went far toward helping keep food on the table and clothes on our backs.

I continued to jerk soda for the Owl Drugstore in Pineville — seven days a week during the summer, then every day after school during the school term, plus full weekends. My pay never rose above the five dollars a week I started out with, but this was enough for me to buy my school lunches, reading material and other growing-up necessities while I attended Bolton High in Alexandria (Pineville at that time had no high school for graduates of its sole grammar school).

As I moved into my junior year at Bolton, I told Mr. Delahoussaye, the owner of Owl Drugstore, that my schoolwork was now so important that I could not spare time for the drugstore any more. He offered to cut my hours in half, while paying me the same wage, so that I only worked every other day after school and only one day on weekends. In view of the increasingly desperate situation at home, I could not refuse this kindness, so I continued to jerk soda and clerk at the Owl, the largest and oldest drugstore in Pineville.

But even then I had no real conception of what the Great Depression was doing to the world and the USA as a whole, and to Pineville citizens in particular. I was certainly unaware of the extent of the difficulty my father was having

19

in bringing home enough money for us to live on. Also about this time, my next older brother, Clyde, was stricken with juvenile diabetes, requiring a considerable, continuous cash outlay for the special medications and foods then in vogue for victims of this life-threatening disease.

Things were not going well at the packing plant as the economy continued to plunge; the time came when Dad was laid off. Like many other businesses in those days, the Rapides plant had to trim costs wherever possible in order to stay afloat and avoid bankruptcy.

By now also, the good friends and neighbors who had supported Mother's Maytag enterprise had reached the limit of their capacity to pay for her home laundry service, so she had to abandon these efforts to supplement the family income.

For a man born on the Texas frontier in 1874, with no education much beyond first grade, who could barely write more than his own name plus necessary figures in elementary addition and subtraction, Dad had accomplished much. However that was not a rarity in the 1800s in his part of the U. S. He loved and cherished his five living children and demonstrated this time and again by special gifts he made to us, which I now know meant depriving himself of much-needed funds; but his family always came first. And because of his lack of education, he was intent on seeing his children attain that goal he had missed out on. It grieved him deeply, visibly, any time he was unable to provide for us.

While we knew Dad loved his family, there was little communication between us. What little we kids learned of his past came from overheard conversations between him and visiting grownups. Impressed at an early age that children should be seen and not heard, we somehow sensed that we were not supposed to ask him questions about his life, past or present.

And since he was the father and husband, in his old-fashioned upbringing he obviously considered it his duty to feed, clothe and house us, without expecting or looking for assistance from us. Had I been able to sit down and have a face-to-face talk with Dad about his problems and what we kids could do to help, I know my life would have been very different from what it became.

Dad's minimal education was not unusual for one

20

born on the Texas frontier in the backwoods of life. But, as he grew up, in addition to learning how to tame wild horses and how to be a carpenter, he also developed one very exceptional talent: he could look at a steer or cow, examine it closely, especially its teeth, and figure within a very few pounds its weight and its approximate age; then he'd buy it and, in good times, make a fair profit. In the days when his abattoir was in full swing, he could do the same with an entire herd of cattle.

This ability was what had motivated his rival to hire him. And when he was laid off by the packing house, Dad still stuck by his cattle experience. He used his old model-T truck to haul, buy, and sell cattle as an independent, in hopes of making a few dollars profit. This worked for a while, but as the economy nationwide continued to slide, the price of beef and cattle on the hoof slid with the trend, down, down, down ... to as low as five cents a pound on the hoof, leaving little room for any worthwhile gain to be made.

So, near the end of my junior year in high school, December 1931, once again we had to move to a less expensive place, abandoning our Pineville home on which Dad could no longer make the mortgage payments. He found a small, unpainted — some called it "shotgun" — frame house in a small community called Tioga, a few miles northeast of Pineville.

When I entered my senior year, which began for me in January 1932, I finally quit my drugstore job. In the teenage dreamworld I occupied, I was still not fully aware of the extreme financial difficulties Dad was having. Working after school had been such a drain on my energy that I was consistently missing one day or more a week from school, for I often stayed home to recuperate.

But as I faced this final year of high school, and since I knew how much Dad wanted us to get a "schooling," I quit work to save my energy so I could spend full time on my studies and activities, which now had become intensely interesting.

Depending on one's birthday, in those days students were allowed to start school at midterm, in January. But I was a midtermer because I had involuntarily skipped the "low 5th" grade in Pineville's grammar school—not because I was exceptionally bright, but because 64 in a classroom was

21

deemed too many students for one teacher to handle. Four of us "brighter" students were directed to skip into the "high 5th," reducing the numbers in the low 5th to a manageable 60 for the one teacher. (When I read about today's classrooms being limited to 30 students, sometimes with one or more teacher assistants, I don't know whether to be envious or just plain puzzled.)

In our new Tioga home, sister Oletta, two years my junior, enrolled at Tioga High School; our youngest, Lela Mae, ten years my junior, was placed in the local grammar school. Technically, I should have attended Tioga High as well, but because of my contacts and hopes at Bolton High and with only a short time to graduate, my advisor, Miss Mary Thornton, persuaded me to continue there. So I stayed in Bolton, and became a reporter on the award-winning high school paper, *Cumtux*.

To remain a student at Bolton wasn't easy. It meant that I had to walk the mile each morning to the community of Kingsville, the end of the line for the school bus which took me through Pineville, across the single bridge over Red River, through the downtown business district of Alexandria, and on near the outskirts of that city to Bolton High.

I discovered that my interests and duties now required that I often remain after school, so many a day I missed the last bus home. This meant I had to walk the full five miles from Bolton to Tioga. But I enjoyed the walk. While striding along, I did a lot of daydreaming about my future, whatever that was to be.

As this spring term began, I bought a secondhand typewriter for five dollars, out of my last earnings from the drugstore. During this term, with the help of the revered Miss Thornton, who was also faculty advisor of *Cumtux*, the school paper, I began to learn the reporter's trade.

I tackled the typewriter touch system on my own time at home, so that I could produce my pieces for the *Cumtux*, all typed neatly. This self-taught typing skill impressed Miss Thornton who began to give me special help in my writing, pointing out errors while commenting and encouraging me on a few basic points of journalism.

Just before school let out for the summer, an event occurred that powerfully influenced my dreams. To my surprise, I was elected editor-in-chief of *Cumtux* for the

22

coming fall semester, my last term. (I will never know for certain, but I will always believe Miss Thornton was the behind-the-scenes string puller who swung enough votes to elect me the *Cumtux* editor.)

Though I did not realize it at the time, I was the first editor ever to come from the "wrong side of the tracks" -- that is, Pineville, on the east side of Red River. I was elated at being elected. And my family was proud of the honor bestowed on me.

Another teacher at Bolton took a special interest in me, my chemistry professor, Mr. Oliphant. He expressed high hopes that by my final senior term I would be representing Bolton High at the annual state rally in chemistry. When he discovered that on many days I didn't have the fifteen cents for my usual lunch of a bottle of Coke and a tuna fish sandwich, he invited me to his home a couple of blocks away to join him and his wife "in a light snack." Light to him, heaven to me; leaving the drugstore had meant many lean days for my belly.

My oldest brother Carl was five years my senior. He was my idol. He could rope cattle, ride horses, go on cattle drives, and guess weights and ages of cattle and horses, just like our father. Carl had long since graduated from high school and was trying to make his own way in the world.

As the summer of 1932 began, it was very near the lowest point of the Great Depression, though we didn't know this at the time. Carl was working at a service station, at a very low salary but still adequate enough to help out some at home. Our diabetic brother, Clyde, whom we always thought had great prospects in life, struggled to earn money, despite his illness, by selling house-to-house men's clothing out of an Ohio mail-order firm. But our neighbors and others were not buying, and he was really too ill to make much of an effort.

About this time I discovered *Liberty* magazine, then a weekly, which featured a short-short story in each issue, and I began trying my hand at writing fiction. I continued this after school let out for the summer. By now, my mind was full of visions of my coming editorship, and one early summer day a great idea dawned: Pineville had no newspaper of any kind. Why not launch a weekly for a brief time during the summer, so that my future staff and I could experiment and be experts by fall?

I broached the idea to my closest friends and classmates: Tommy Kohara, son of a popular photography shop owner; Rollo Lawrence, the Pineville mayor's son; and Delos Don Gayer, son of a highly regarded Baptist preacher. They agreed to the venture, and forthwith we began to scout around for a print shop in Pineville.

We found one, one that actually had a Mergenthaler Linotype, the typesetting machine that had revolutionized the world of printing. Many an hour I watched in fascination as its operator touched keys and levers, while it clicked and moved its molten metal into a line of type to transform words into the magic of a final printed page.

The owner was enthusiastic about the idea of a newspaper, even a weekly, and we quickly struck a deal that we thought we could handle. No doubt he saw it as a permanent product that he could continue himself, after we had broken ground. The only other local paper was the *Daily Town Talk*, published across the river in Alexandria, the parish seat. More than once he said to me, "Maybe Pineville's time has come."

We agreed on the deadline for copy for the first issue and began knocking on doors to collect the munificent sum of ten cents per subscriber, which our printer friend had assured us would, along with advertisements we had lined up, cover the number of issues we planned.

I stayed up late the night of June 21, at the service station where brother Carl was working, to listen to the radio broadcast of the big prizefight between Sharkey and Schmeling. I then wrote it up as the lead story and the next day handed it to our printer along with other items, for him to set in type on his magic machine.

I waited, and waited, and waited, but the magic was gone from this secondhand, broken-down typesetting machine. Its performance was erratic and unpredictable. Like the Great Depression surrounding us, it had hit bottom.

Day after day I visited the shop, until finally, in despair, the printer turned to me and said, "I just can't get it to working on a steady enough basis to do what is necessary for a regular paper," and he handed back our items, obviously as unhappy about it as I. After all, he had to fall back to setting type by hand for his regular printing — a

24

tedious, time-consuming task.

I passed the sad news of the demise of our enterprise along to my buddies, who went on the sadder trail of refunding the deposits to our subscribers. Then I retreated to Tioga for the remainder of the summer, helping Mother tend the remaining vegetables in the little garden that adjoined our house, typing every day page after page of what I thought was a novel, or a short story. I even sent a short-short or two to *Liberty*, and reaped my first stereotyped rejection slips. A short story submitted to *Amazing Stories* also drew a rejection though its editor, John W. Campbell, Jr., was kind enough to include a few encouraging remarks.

I began to look forward eagerly to the coming school term in September, until the day summer was almost gone, when the roof fell in.

I happened to overhear Mother ask Dad for some grocery money. I saw him pull out a single, wrinkled and torn dollar bill, hand it to her, turn, and leave the house without saying a word. I watched him with his battered cowboy hat, grim-faced, get into the old model-T truck, set the hand brake, the spark and gas levers, get out and turn the crank, hop in and slowly rattle off.

For the first time my eyes opened all the way, and the full extent of our situation dawned on me: it was desperate. For the first time I began to consider the fact that three of us, my two sisters and I, were about to enter a new school year.

Normally, this meant new clothes, and though the famous Huey Long, when governor of the state (later, a U. S. Senator), had done away with the need for us to buy our school books, nevertheless there would be other school supplies, notebooks, writing materials, and so on, we would have to purchase on our own.

I didn't mind doing without new clothes and was not ashamed of the clean patches on my pants and the elbows of my shirts and sweater. More and more of my classmates, particularly those from the Pineville side of Red River, were similarly attired. But I fully anticipated there would be some unusual expenses connected with my job as editor of *Cumtux*.

Should I return to work at the drugstore? *Could* I return? And if I could, how would it affect the time I would need to handle my extra *Cumtux* duties?

When I had given the drugstore owner notice of my

25

leaving, he had tried to talk me into staying on with him. He would even help me go to college, he said, and I would become a licensed pharmacist! And that, he argued, would keep me off the front lines "should we ever get into a war again." (And this was almost ten years before Pearl Harbor.) He also hadn't hesitated to point out that the two other drugstores in town were both owned by former employees of his. In other words, my future prospects were bright if I would choose to become a pharmacist.

But I hesitated about going back to him now; I had refused the temptation to become a druggist, and also I suspected that he had long since hired a replacement soda jerker. And besides, teenagers think only of going forward — not backwards.

I deliberated intently as I bent over picking the last crop of beans in the garden, the last cabbages and the last cantaloupes, which, along with the other garden produce, had sustained us through much of the summer. I went into the house for a heart-to-heart talk with Mother. No mention was made of the shattered state of Dad's income, luckily supplemented by brother Carl, but I raised the question as to whether I should look for after-school work.

Mother paused a long, thoughtful moment before she spoke, then said that Dad was so proud of what I was to do, that he wanted me to spend all the time necessary doing it and would not want me to hurt my chances by spending time working. She also pointed out the many days I had missed school from exhaustion due to holding down even the part-time drugstore job.

I pondered and brooded a few more days. Time was getting short, as school was to start again all too soon. The fact that my favorite brother Carl had previously left home after he had finished high school, and had gone off to Texas looking for work, may have been in the back of my mind. But my teenage mentality neglected to recall that he then had come back, to work in his hometown. And, of course, Dad was on his own as early as thirteen, though he had drifted rather than run away to do so.

The decisive moment — the straw that broke the camel's back — came by accident when I stumbled across a stack of unpaid bills addressed to Dad. On examining them closely, I sat down hard. For the first time, I seriously, consciously, concentrated on the situation my family was in. These were not first-time billings, but second, third and final demands for payment. My father was faced with a financial impossibility, as I now perceived all too clearly.

Brother Clyde was still fighting severe diabetes and needed a constant supply of medicine and special foods. And to serve as the editor of Bolton's award-winning high school newspaper, I was expected to make a certain number of official trips out of town. The vegetable garden was all gone; everything edible in it was completely picked out. There were no other sources of income in sight that would fund my schooling, over and above the minimum needed to keep our family alive.

How could I participate in coming school events without funds, without at least a few necessities, some spending money for food, meetings and social affairs that, as an editor, I was supposed to attend?

It was then that I concluded that my final term at Bolton High would put too great a financial burden on my father, whose earning power had shrunk to a miniscule $3, $4, or $5 per week — many weeks, nothing. Financial burden? Where there are no finances at all, can there be such a thing as a financial burden?

In these Great Depression days, there was no governmental assistance, and private charities, where they existed, had exhausted most of their resources. Personal bankruptcy was considered by most people to be a demeaning, shameful if not dishonest way of escaping creditors. Dad would never take that way out, I knew. And the only relatives were Mother's and they lived many miles away.

Having reached that conclusion, what should I do?

With immense regret at giving up the opportunity to be editor of the school paper, I made the decision to run away, to thereby reduce the drain on my father's thin wallet. I even had visions of sending money home from afar. In one fantasy, I would get to Dallas, Texas, headquarters of *Holland's*, a popular magazine in the southern states, and convince someone there to take me on as a writer.

Little did I perceive at the time that I was personally challenging the Great Depression with my only proven, saleable talent being a soda jerker, or possibly a dishwasher, though how much talent the latter took was certainly subject

27

to question. And though I hadn't graduated from high school, I had ten and a half years of schooling as opposed to my dad's one or two years at most. And he had succeeded at an even younger age than I. He was about thirteen by the time he was earning a living breaking in and selling wild horses. At eighteen, he was learning how to carpenter.

Could I at sixteen, with a better education, equal or do better than my dad at thirteen? The contest was not with my father; my challenge was to survive in the Great Depression. I was confident I could do it. Sixteen-year-olds don't think of losing or retreating; they may think poorly but they think BIG.

After all the lights were out in our frame house and everyone was asleep, I arose in the dark, put on my clothes and fetched up the traveling bundle I had hidden earlier. I placed a note, that I had prepared, on top of my pillow. The message said:

"Please don't worry, but I'm leaving to look for work. We don't have the money for me to go back to school. I'm going to Texas and will write you from there. Love, Alma."

I signed it with the name I had been known by for the first sixteen years of my life, Alma. As I stepped out onto the highway headed away from Tioga, I left this name behind forever, along with my life in Louisiana.

The author returning to Tioga, Louisiana, and the house he ran away from.

28

Teenage years are a critical period of increased awareness of the real world, when a youngster's consciousness is most vulnerable to stress and pull from many forces — not all of them benign.

—(The Author)

Chapter 3

LITTLE   LIVER   PILLS

After midnight on Monday, September 12, 1932, in the Great Depression, I walked along U.S. Highway 71 in Louisiana, putting as many miles as possible between me and home before daylight. I was headed northwest toward Shreveport, with a hope that anyone searching for me would assume my destination was Houston, Texas, where a sister of Mother's lived, and the area of Texas where brother Carl had gone.

In the dark of early morning I plodded steadily along the highway trying to focus all my thoughts on the future and to avoid thinking of the past I had just severed. I was determined to curb any negative thoughts.

I had clipped off a good dozen miles by the time day began to break. Rosy hues from sunlight reflecting off a wealth of clouds greeted the dawn, just as majestic and beautiful as a Louisiana sunset.

As the sun finally peeped through to warm the pavement, various vehicles began to appear on the highway. Most were farmers' trucks or old jalopies, but a few belonged to businessmen and salesmen, I found out, as one after another would stop and give me a ride for a few miles at least.

The road led to Bossier City. Hitchhiking was not a problem in those troubled times, as it was not unusual for young boys to be hitching a ride as I was doing. The kind drivers who picked me up were well aware of the many homes with meager larders, little money, and no immediate prospects for the future.

To the curious, as almost all were, I explained my journey by stating I was a high school graduate, unable to find work at home, and was going to visit relatives in Texas with hopes of better luck there. No one questioned this story and seemed happy to give me a lift "as fer as I'm goin'."

There was just the suggestion of an early autumn nip in the air as I was dropped off by one driver after another. After passing through the town of Colfax, with its locally famous "flaming fountain" (water, with a mixture of natural gas that had been lit and burned continuously), I made fairly good time; practically every vehicle headed my way seemed willing to give me a ride whenever I gave the thumb signal.

As we rode along chatting, I observed the scenery, the farms and farmhouses that bordered the road. I could detect no signs here of the Depression. There were a lot of unpainted, wooden shacks for tenant farmers and small landholders, but this was nothing new in my memory of Louisiana. Some of the shacks were obviously vacant, but this also seemed the norm in this part of the world.

In the fields I could see men and women harvesting corn by hand. The usually verdant countryside was turning brown, with the end of summer near, but there was no sign yet of the terrible dust clouds that would later devastate Oklahoma, and the high plains of Texas, and other midwestern areas.

As noon approached, my last ride let me off near a small country store. Having had no breakfast and now feeling the pangs of hunger, I went in and from my small hoard of money bought a can of sardines and a loaf of bread: total cost, twenty cents. This was more than it would have been in a city or town, but normal for a backwoods grocery.

I intended this purchase to last me all day, for this first day away from home, but growing teenage boys need lots of food. I would become well aware of this truth before day's end.

30

Finally, after a succession of short rides during the heat of early afternoon, my last one brought me to Bossier City, my first destination. There was still some daylight left, time to make some moves in job hunting.

I was lugging a bundle of personal possessions which included several short stories and what I considered to be a short novel. I naturally regarded this treasure trove to be substantial evidence that I was an accomplished writer and author.

My first target in Bossier City was the local newspaper office where I hoped to sell myself and my professional products. I actually got to meet the editor-publisher personally. He was not unkind, but sorry, no openings. Times were tough, he said — as if I didn't know.

So I tried a different approach: how about letting me write short items, the fillers that occupy the spaces at the end of articles and stories? Or even sell these as reading tidbits on restaurant menus, which I had noticed his firm printed? He seemed to perk up at my second suggestion but thoughtfully shook his head and said that market was not profitable enough in these days of the Depression.

I wandered around the rest of that afternoon looking for work of any kind — without success. Even in the depths of the Great Depression (as in all other times) there seemed to be a demand for dishwashers. There were signs in Bossier City restaurant windows advertising for dishwashers all right, but they read like this: "Dishwasher wanted — only college graduates need apply."

Not believing these words about college graduates, I entered several cafes to inquire personally and always got the same reply: "We mean it, sonny. We are helping those who have finished college and can't find any other work."

As I walked the streets, I passed many more vacant, boarded-up businesses than I had seen in Pineville or Alexandria. There were also more men and boys, with bundles on their backs, shaggy-looking with dirty clothes full of patches and torn spots. I felt that I was better dressed, cleaner-looking than many, which gave me some degree of confidence.

At the end of this first day, dead tired, mentally and physically, I spent fifteen cents on a hardy supper of a hamburger and a glass of sweet milk (our name for milk that wasn't buttermilk), then searched for a warm place to put down my bundle. This roll consisted of half of a light blanket, a bar of soap and a face towel — more like a rag — plus the aforementioned hoard of my writings.

I found my haven at a local gymnasium I had passed earlier while exploring Bossier City. The gym contained a boxing ring surrounded by a scattering of several rows of chairs for spectators. The place was wide open, to enable participants in the coming Golden Glove matches to practice, and I casually read a notice on the bulletin board that said all such contestants would be rewarded with a free meal after their bouts, winners and losers alike.

I found a dark corner, well out of sight, where I could evade detection — or so I presumed. And despite the buzz and hum of boxers filling the gym, I was so exhausted that I fell asleep quickly.

As daylight and a morning sun peeking through a small window warmed me awake, I glanced up to see a man staring pensively down at me. As soon as I could gather my wits enough to recall where I was, I figured that as I was an intruder I would most likely be kicked out. But that was not to be.

"You must be here to try out for the Golden Gloves?" the man half asked, half stated.

Thinking quickly, I nodded yes. This was apparently all he needed to know. Other than asking my name and where I was from, he made no further personal inquiries. I gave my middle name, Duval, as my first name, which few ever knew me by back home, but I lied again about being a high school graduate. I feared that if he knew that I had half a school year to go before graduating, he would probably turn me over to the police as a runaway — or so my thoughts ran. As it was, he volunteered to give me some pointers on boxing.

With the help of this kind stranger, I filled out the required forms and was scheduled to box in the first tryouts only two nights away. At the same time, I was automatically matched with a boxer in my weight class, who had previously registered. I was so intrigued at his name, Onionhead, that I did not pay attention to the information about his height.

That day I put on boxing gloves for the first time in

my life, and under the watchful eye of my benefactor worked the punching bag. I had a guilty feeling at the start, remembering Dad's preaching against boxing, but this went away when I recalled that each participant would be rewarded with a free meal after the fight. I would be working for my food, and this contrived reasoning mollified my guilt feelings somewhat.

As I worked to master this art that I never thought I would be engaged in, my sponsor demonstrated how to keep up my guard and gave me a few other pointers a boxer should know in order to survive, though he failed to mention Tunney's bicycle stratagem.

I left the gym a couple of times to eat, spending from my small hoard of nickels and dimes. And again this night I found a corner in the gym and slept soundly without fear of ejection.

The day of my first match dawned and I decided to spend much of it on the west side of Red River, in the larger city of Shreveport. There I made the rounds of restaurants and cafes, looking for dishwashing jobs.

As I passed the occasional drugstore, I would ask about a sodajerk job, confident that my three years' experience at the busiest drugstore in Pineville surely qualified me. As with the cafes, my talents were not in demand at drugstores either.

By afternoon I wound up at the public library. Since my eventual desire was to go to Texas, I now initiated a procedure that I have since adhered to whenever I enter a new city: I read the city maps, memorizing the main roads and railroads leading into and out of the city in all directions.

Having done this and feeling there was still some purpose and direction to my life, some hope for the future, I returned to Bossier City and the gym. I spent the remaining time in the company of my sponsor, who gave me a final review and checkout before my initiation into the boxing bout described earlier where I had managed to best Kid Onionhead of Shreveport two rounds out of three.

Though that had been my first boxing experience, I had been involved in a real fistfight once before in my life. It occurred at the old swimming hole upstream from where a little brook, that we called Clear Run, entered the northern boundary of Dad's slaughterhouse acreage.

33

One sunny summer afternoon the swimming hole was filled with the usual group of naked white boys when some black boys showed up. Instead of waiting for us to leave, as was the custom, or going downstream to a less desirable spot, one of the blacks began to undress as if he were preparing to dive into our "white" hole while we were still in it. One of my classmates, taller and heavier than I, was incensed at such a breach of custom and began cursing and ordering the blacks to leave.

To me this seemed so unfair, especially since we were in the process of departing anyhow, that I flung myself in a sudden rage at my white companion with a flurry of flying fists. This surprise attack from someone with a reputation for being shy and reserved caught him so off guard that he instantly threw up his arms and yelled "I quit! I quit!"

That fistfight victory resulted from the same kind of red rage that had triggered my onslaught in round two of my match with Kid Onionhead. Clearly, a person under the influence of great rage can perform unbelievable physical feats.

My concern in the one-week interval between bout one with Onionhead and our grudge match was to find a daytime job. My coaching sessions with my sponsor were held in the evenings, and though he wasn't pressing me, I continued to conceal from him my exact circumstances. He apparently was under the impression that I had money or was getting money from home or from nearby relatives. I did not try to enlighten him.

The second day following bout one, down to my last dime, I got my first break. It was a notice in a circular seeking boys and men to deliver free samples of Argotane Little Liver Pills from door to door in Shreveport and vicinity. I appeared at the designated spot in time to be hired. It was exhilarating finally to be doing something to earn some money, and the pay was great — a whole dollar for one day's work.

The day was a short one, only eight hours long. My fortunes had turned the corner. Was this a step on the way to taking care of myself, perhaps even sending a little extra money back home?

Eight hours of jumping off a truck with a handful of pill samples and dropping one at the door of each house in a block, then back to the truck, move to the next block, repeat

34

the performance, hour after hour, so that it could almost be done with my eyes closed.

Although I was used to staying on my feet for twelve hours and more when jerking soda at the drugstore on a weekend, at the end of my first day delivering Argotane samples my feet hurt. But I was elated when the crew manager put a dollar bill in my hands and said, "See you tomorrow."

With my first day's pay, I splurged, an entire twenty-five-cent dinner, complete with dessert and a bottle of a local soft drink that I have seen nowhere else, called "Aunt Ida." (The same firm also promoted a drink called "Uncle Joe" which I tried later.) And I added a cheap pair of undershorts from Woolworth's to my bundle.

Again I slept in the gym, for free. No one seemed to mind, as the word was out that I would be there to fight in a coming revenge battle. Boxing was indeed popular in Bossier City — and Golden Glove boxers were granted privileges!

After my second day on the Argotane job, when the crew manager placed a dollar bill in my outstretched hand, I was so overcome by a feeling of financial security that I bought a full evening meal once again and followed it by taking in a musical stage show, my first such event.

That senseless adolescent act still left me with enough money for a healthy breakfast of bacon and eggs the next morning and a hurried hamburger for lunch while hopping from block to block with Little Liver Pill samples in my bag.

The third day was much like the first two, except that I had an unhappy encounter with a small, yapping dog which managed to bite hard enough through my thin trousers to break the skin on my leg before the owner could call him off. The crew manager immediately stopped the canvassing and took me to a nearby drugstore, where the druggist washed off the bite, put on Mercurochrome and a bandage. (That was a very dangerous treatment for a dog bite. In later years I learned more about rabies. Then, in my innocence, I thought everything was hunky-dory. And the good Lord above kept it that way for me.)

At the end of that day, the crew manager paid us off with the usual dollar bill while saying good-by. He was moving on with his samples to the next big city. Thus abruptly ended my juvenile dream of being on the path to self-sufficiency.

I clutched that last dollar bill and vowed I'd make it last. Alas, the growing pains of a sixteen-year-old caused the dollar to vanish that night and the days following, swallowed in substantial meals while I searched in vain for another job of any kind.

The final days before the second fight introduced me to really sharp pains of hunger. I was completely out of money. No food passed my lips. My stomach must have shrunk, although I continued to drink ample quantities of water in an effort to fill the growing void.

Finally, the day of the grudge match arrived. The hunger pains now had begun to subside somewhat, or else I had learned how to ignore them. So all that day I remained at the gym, went through the motions of shadow boxing and working the punching bag as well as I could, and thought about the nice, juicy steak that would be my reward after the bout — whether I won or lost.

My sponsor showed up an hour before fight time. He must have discerned something in my face. Gauntness? He asked if I had been eating properly. I thought it was time to level with him and did so, up to a point. I still concealed the fact that I was a runaway and a school dropout.

I told him I felt strong, however (a false sense that people get just from drinking lots of water), and ready and able to go through with the fight. After all, my reward would be that big steak dinner afterwards. He said very little as he continued to help me prepare for the bout.

I gulped down a cooling glass of water before I marched into the arena to take my post in the ring. This time the announcer gave a somewhat longer introduction, explaining the nature of this unofficial bout.

The crowd hushed. The bell clanged for round one.

I intended to jump quickly to the center of the ring as I had done before, but this time around it was a different story. I had barely risen and taken one step forward when, lightning quick, Kid Onionhead dashed all the way across the ring and landed one blow with his right fist alongside my left temple.

I floated gently down to the canvas, the floor of the ring, in a delicious haze. I was not entirely out, because I

36

heard someone shout (to me, it seemed a murmur) "The kid hasn't eaten in three days." It could only have been my sponsor, though I couldn't recognize the voice through my mental fog.

The next instant a white towel flew from my corner into the ring, an automatic signal that the fight was over. I did not have to be counted out; the bout ended when the towel was thrown. That was how I learned what the expression "to throw in the towel" means.

Thus ignominiously ended what probably was the shortest fight in history — or at least in unofficial Golden Glove history.

Thanks to the considerate sponsors of the event, both Onionhead and I were still invited to partake in the free meal offered to the official participants.

And boy! Did that steak dinner ever taste great! After all, only one spot in my entire body was hurting — a spot that interfered not a whit with the movement of my jaws as I made that "free" steak journey down to befriend my lonesome belly!

"The circus and circus people are very special ..."
— **Harry Hertzberg**

Chapter 4

HAPPY BRRRR THDAY!

Following my historic one-punch knockout, two things brought a glow back into my body. First, that delicious, filling, steak dinner, more enjoyable than the first one as I now ached in only one nonessential place. Second, a most surprising gesture came from my erstwhile opponent: Kid Onionhead strode over to my table, grabbed my right hand and shook it vigorously.

He looked a very different person from my grim ring adversary. In fact, he was smiling broadly as he invited me to his home for dinner the next evening! Still engaged in the unexpected thrill of actually enjoying my steak, I mumbled a "Thank you" but made a noncommittal answer to the invitation. He gave my shoulder a friendly pat and departed.

Had I not been a runaway, I probably would have accepted Onionhead's kind invitation. But, in olden days, a teenager in my situation had to be wary of people with good intentions, as well as of the law. I risked being forcibly returned, or at least thought I did, to the home I'd run away from. Actually, as the Great Depression deepened, this rule loosened considerably. There were simply too many such cases for undermanned police departments to be concerned with every derelict youngster found on their turf. It took me a while to grasp this change in the situation.

In failing to accept Onionhead's thoughtful offer, I lost my chance to learn his full name. Of more import to me, it left unanswered that question that has nagged me for years: Did Onionhead simply use a poor choice of words when he urged me to take it easy? After all, he also was a teenager, and perhaps his only concern was to lessen the battering that I was obviously taking in that first round? Now, I'll never know for certain.

Neither my sponsor nor anyone else mentioned an appearance in further Golden Glove bouts, and by this time I had positively lost any desire to enter a boxing ring again. I did take advantage though of sleeping free in my customary corner of the gym that night.

The next morning I read a newspaper story about the Hagenbeck-Wallace Circus scheduled to perform in Shreveport that day, headlining Clyde Beatty "battling 40 ferocious lions and tigers." Beatty's act (I would meet him one day) did not entice me. The paragraph that caught my attention was "Helpers needed to water elephants and for other chores around the circus." Another big dollar-day in my life?

Full of youthful hope, I made my way to the circus grounds, found the man in charge of hiring and was granted permission to "water the elephants." I didn't know enough to ask in advance what my pay would be. Instead, I fantasized again of getting at least a dollar.

No time was wasted in putting me to work at my assigned task. Within minutes I was hard at it. All that morning and afternoon I lugged heavy buckets of sloshing water to those bottomless pits called elephants, whose thirst seemed unquenchable. I never realized until then that water could be so heavy.

While I tended to the water wants of these leviathans, the sounds and sights of the circus coming to life went on all around me. The main tent was the big project, and when the center poles were erected, some of my elephant friends lent a hand, that is, their long, tough trunk, to speed things along. They were very good at what they did, so I kept right on bringing them their water reward, to be replaced no doubt later that evening by tons of peanuts from circus customers.

40

Finally through, I went to draw my pay. It was a dollar, all right, but in the form of merchandise! I was handed two "free" general admission tickets to the night performance in the big top, each worth fifty cents.

There is a magic about circuses, carnivals, the smell of sawdust, the sounds of wild animals, enticing scenes on giant canvases, tantalizing odors from fast food stands and cotton candy counters, all intermingled with the barking of ticket sellers at all the sideshows and at the main tent, the "big top." Any other time, I would have jumped at the chance to enjoy the show. But I had been to circuses before with my family, and on this September day I had no wish to see one again. I wanted food money instead.

The immediate problem was how to convert my circus tickets into cash? The solution was surprisingly simple. Walk through a poor section of the city and yell, "Cheap tickets to the circus, half price!"

Though I had to explain to prospective purchasers how I had acquired the tickets, to my intense relief as well as amazement, they went quickly for half price. With little to brighten their daily lives, poor people love the affordable excitement of circuses. So, once again, I managed to get enough money for a decent meal with some change left over.

The circus tents were pitched in vacant fields on what was then the outskirts of Shreveport, near U.S. Highway 80 heading west, not far from a railroad. I was pointed in the direction I now was determined to go more than ever. I figured my luck was used up so far as Shreveport and Bossier City were concerned. If one were to consider my appearance in these two cities as Round One in my battle with the Great Depression, I'd concede that I lost this round, at least on points.

By the time the circus tickets were changed into cash, and supper was safely behind, it was dark. The gym was too far away to sponge another night there. Besides, somehow I couldn't imagine being as welcome as before.

Fortunately I had brought my belongings along with me. For a couple of hours I wandered through the gathering throngs of circus goers, inhaling the overpowering odors from the hot dog and hamburger stands, drinking in the numerous smells and noises that can only come from a traveling circus. Yes, I liked the excitement of it all, under

41

normal circumstances. But, being a runaway teenager, there was no way I could call these normal circumstances.

Finally, tired of walking around and merely looking, I searched for a place to bed down for the rest of the night. A deserted warehouse a couple of blocks from the circus grounds provided the answer. It was so close that sounds, lights and even smells of the many concessions and sideshows that surrounded the big top continued to reach me as I removed my shoes. Otherwise, fully clothed, I lay down for the night on a wooden porch sheltered by a roof.

My last conscious thought as I drifted off into restless slumber was that tomorrow, September 23, would be my seventeenth birthday.

The noise and music and circus aromas continued to penetrate my half-sleep for a while, followed by a long silence. Then the rumbling and roar of trucks and caged animals dimly pierced my exhausted consciousness. Sometime later I sensed movement of a person or people, and marveled subconsciously that I could detect all this activity from some two blocks away.

As daylight greeted me on my seventeenth birthday, I reached outside my short blanket and groped near my feet where I had placed my shoes. No shoes! Alarmed, I sat up and looked around carefully, but clearly no shoes were in sight.

It then struck me. Someone had taken them during the night. It must have been the person whose movement I had sensed in my sleep. A shoe thief! Unheard of in my life! What a dirty trick! Had it been some circus roustabout, or just some tramp passing by?

At that moment I muttered to myself, "I'm seventeen today, and my feet are as bare as the day I was born. Someday, maybe, I'll laugh about this."

There seemed to be no alternative but to rebind my pack, swing it over my shoulder and step out onto cold pavement. My naked feet (I had no socks) immediately sent up a message that confirmed summer was over on this very day and that fall had officially arrived. I made my barefoot way the one block to the highway with little difficulty. After a while, numbness from cold obscured the pain.

At the highway I automatically stuck out my right hand and thumb in the traditional signal; I was no longer a neophyte in the art of hitchhiking. Besides, drivers in the Great Depression were quite considerate about giving lifts to strangers, especially young ones with no shoes on.

Sure enough, soon a genial older man in a pickup truck slowed down almost to a stop and yelled, "Hop in!"

By now I had revised my stock answer to questions about my destination: "I'm on my way to Fort Worth, to visit a relative there," a fabrication I continued to use as long as my journey lay in that direction.

I had selected Fort Worth because a pen pal I'd developed through my science fiction reading lived there. I had no intention of showing up on his doorstep. But I had conceived a plan of putting his return address on any letters I mailed home, so as to thwart any efforts to have me picked up as a runaway. This fear diminished completely with the passage of days and weeks, with no police authorities making any move toward me.

I had already written and asked my pen pal to serve as a mail drop and forwarding service, though these terms were unknown to me at that time. The arrangement was that I would write a letter home, place it in a stamped, addressed envelope and seal it, then enclose that in a larger envelope and mail it to my friend to forward. This plan worked well enough to satisfy me that I was getting word to the family that its runaway member was okay, while continuing to conceal my exact whereabouts.

The friendly driver was a jolly farmer-rancher from East Texas. After satisfying himself that he was being a Good Samaritan to a bona fide, barefoot pilgrim, he jabbered ceaselessly about his homestead, prices of produce, the hard times, and so on and so on. He was returning to his farm just over the border in Texas, after delivering a load of produce in Shreveport. He laughed sympathetically when I told him how I'd lost my shoes.

The miles passed slowly. His truck's top speed was no more than a jolting thirty miles an hour. As we crossed the border into Texas, for the first time I began to chuckle aloud at my situation and told the driver that it was funny that I was entering the great state of Texas completely barefoot on my seventeenth birthday. He joined me in merriment. Laughter doesn't fill an empty stomach, but it does wonders in keeping one's spirits up.

A little beyond the state line, as we neared a railroad crossing, he brought his truck to a groaning halt, waved his weather-beaten hand at a footpath leading through the brush toward the railroad and told me to follow that trail. It led to a place where there was an ample supply of shoes to pick from, he assured me. With a gentle pat on my shoulder, he bade me good luck and farewell.

Somewhat mystified, I nevertheless thanked him and entered the pathway. Half a block from the highway it ended at an open space under a railroad trestle. In the shade of a nearby lone oak tree, a roughly dressed man sat comfortably on a log, using a long stick to prod a small fire under a pot of some kind. It struck me at once. This was a hobo jungle, a camp used by hoboes and tramps following the railroads, reputed to be their favorite mode of free travel.

The hobo gave me a long stare that started at the top of my head and ended at my feet. My unshod extremities brought a friendly grin to his face. He pointed over his shoulder and said, "Take your pick from that pile, sonny."

Behind him, under the partial protection of the railroad trestle, was a mountain of discarded men's shoes! All sizes, shapes, colors and conditions, but no matched pairs, of course.

I put my bundle down and began to paw through the huge pile. Within a few minutes I found an acceptable fit in a left-foot shoe, black, with no hole in the sole. Matching it with a right-foot shoe close to the same color was harder, but eventually I succeeded. I was satisfied. What I now had was actually better than what I had lost to the midnight shoe thief.

As I returned to the fire, I saw that a second hobo had now joined the first and was in the process of throwing peeled potatoes in the pot. They both made room for me on the log, as the first man said, "Nice fit, sonny." I nodded agreement. A long silence followed.

I wondered. Should I talk with these people? Should I tell them where I'm going, where I've come from? Talk only when talked to, answer only a specific question, I decided. Without guidance I had stumbled onto one of the correct codes of behavior in the hobo jungle, at least in the days of the Great Depression. Within hours I would learn, emphatically, that one is wise to observe this code.

I had decided to give the railroad a try at reaching my

next destination. Fate had brought me here, so I wanted to see where fate would next lead me. Besides, trains traveled through the night whereas hitchhiking only worked well in broad daylight.

The hours dragged slowly by. Other hoboes joined the party throughout the day, with very little talking. These were grim, silent men, most of them down on their luck, out of a job. They asked me only one question: "Going east or west?" "West," I replied and was thankful that was sufficient for these mostly silent men.

As an afternoon freight train slowly passed, heading east, the numbers thinned as half the men swung bundles over shoulders, went up the steep bank to the railroad bed and at the first passing open door, swung easily into the boxcar. A few turned and casually waved a hand. So that was how it was done.

At the time I didn't question the fact that half the men were headed east looking for a better life, while the other half were going west for the same reason. Something was surely wrong with job hunting in our country. Has it improved at all, with the passing years?

By now the hobo stew began to smell more enticing, as some of the men had added carrots and some kind of meat to the common pot. I had nothing to contribute, but by now I was learning to live with hunger pangs.

As the sun began to set, the hoboes produced bowls and spoons from their packs and ate silently. No one made a move to offer me anything. Had they done so I had made up my mind to say, "No thanks, I'm not hungry," or "I ate a big lunch."

I wasn't sure of the nature of all the ingredients in that stew, and I wasn't yet hungry enough to risk that particular unknown. I figured someone else would have to describe the magic of hobo stew to the world.

At twilight there came the sound I had been awaiting, the slowly increasing rumble of a westbound freight. Passenger trains had passed, bringing no stir from the gathered hoboes. At this jungle no one seemed interested in traveling faster than a freight.

As the westbound came nearer, most of the remaining hoboes slowly gathered their belongings. I followed suit. Then the hoboes spaced themselves at the edge of bushes on

45

the steep slope, putting a boxcar distance between them. I went to the extreme end of the line, the better to observe the exact procedure to safely board the train. I was old enough and cautious enough to know what happens when a boxcar rolls across a careless person's legs.

The train engine finally passed, slowly picking up speed on a long incline. As it went by the first waiting "passenger," he stood up, put his bundle into his left hand and deftly swung his body into the first empty boxcar that came along. Others down the line were doing the same. I spotted my target near the end of the train, an open flatcar filled with a load of what appeared to be pairs of train wheels mounted on axles. I caught the steps, swung up, and found myself staring into the face of another youth about my age. This particular flatcar turned out to be loaded not only with train wheels but also with a horde of free passengers!

I clambered among the wheels, which were stacked in about three levels, until I found an unoccupied dark spot in the very middle of the flatcar, completely hidden from view from any direction. I crawled down into it and made myself as comfortable as possible by pulling my half blanket around me as far as it would stretch.

As the train picked up speed, I gradually dozed off, lulled by the rhythm of the rails, the clickety-clack, clickety-clack of train wheels hitting each rail juncture. At last, I was really heading west.

The miles — and the hours — slowly rolled by. I knew the freight train was not going very fast, but it beat hitchhiking, I thought. It seemed to stop at every little crossroad and village and, time after time, pulled onto sidetracks to allow passage for zooming passenger trains, to uncouple a boxcar or two, or to hook on a new one.

But "catching the train" had been so simple. No wonder it was so popular. What a great way to travel. It was free and I was traveling even while sleeping!

Hours passed. Then the freight began to slow again. It was still dark, but the faint glow of a false dawn informed me that daylight was not far behind. We slowed down to a crawl, I heard the sound of switches being thrown, and we rolled onto yet another sidetrack. But this time I heard no passenger train coming. We came to a complete stop. Other than the subdued chuffing of an idling locomotive, there was dead silence.

Suddenly, out of the dark came one of the harshest voices I have ever heard, "All right, you bums. Get off this train right NOW!"

I heard shuffling as men and boys moved around me. For reasons I cannot fathom even now, I stayed put in my warm cocoon, making no movement or sound of any kind. Perhaps it was because I was not yet fully awake. It all seemed like a dream.

"All you bums. Off! NOW! I've got a gun covering every one of you, and I'm not afraid to use it on you freeloaders!" yelled the harsh voice.

Sounds of rustling movement continued as more and more men and boys scrambled out of hiding places on my flatcar and from the boxcars along the line.

By now I was wide awake and pondering if I should join the exodus, but might not my belated response bode ill for me? Again I heard that hard, harsh voice bark, "Line up, you bums, and face me." Feet shuffled into position, still with no one but Harsh-voice speaking.

It was at this moment that I got up the courage to peek out on the scene from my place of concealment. In the early dawn's light I saw at least two dozen men and youths standing in a double line facing one man, the harsh-voiced one. I could see a glint of light from the barrel of the revolver he held in his right hand.

Should I join them?

Just on the point of getting up, something happened that kept me glued in place. Harsh-voice pointed his gun at a burly individual and ordered, "All right, YOU, yes, you, you bum. Give me your wallet — and no funny moves, any of you."

Burly slowly reached into his left hip pocket and pulled out a wallet.

"Hand it over!" Harsh-voice ordered, brandishing the revolver. He took the wallet with his left hand, flipped it over, expertly pulled out some bills, and then threw the wallet on the ground in front of the burly man, and said, more quietly: "Okay, you've paid for some of your way, at least! Get the hell out of here and don't any of you come back! Hear!"

That was enough to sway me to stay very quietly

47

exactly where I was, until the last of the hoboes had disappeared and the yard bull, Harsh-voice, had gone in the direction of the engine. After a few minutes passed, I said good-by to the train, jumping as quietly as I could down onto the ground on the opposite side of the scene I had just witnessed. I had had enough of a free ride on the rails.

Ahead were lights of a town or city, so I started walking slowly towards them. It was now light enough to distinguish more and more of the shapes. As far as my eyes could see, there were oil derricks dotting the horizon in every direction. Many were filling the air with the distinctive noise of pumping black gold to the surface, oil to fuel America's machines.

I suddenly bumped into someone headed in the same direction and recognized him as one of those recent "free-loaders" lined up by the harsh-voiced "dick," the railroad detective.

"Where are we?" I blurted.

"I think it's Gladewater, sonny, an oil boomtown. Looks like we're both headed there. My name is Fred," he added, sticking out his right hand.

"Mine's Duval," I responded. This was the longest conversation, and the friendliest, I'd carried on with a fellow hobo.

"Where're you from?" I managed to squeak out, thinking it was time for me to get friendly, too.

His reaction to this question was totally unexpected. Fred wheeled around, fiercely grasped my shoulders with both hands, looked me straight in the eyes and sternly commanded: "Don't ever, *ever*, ask a hobo where he's *from*. Understand? It's *none* of your business!"

He released his grasp and resumed his walking toward town, as if nothing unusual had happened. I partially regained my composure while mentally adding yet another item to the growing list of my travel learnings. It's okay to ask where he's going but don't ever ask a hobo where he's *from*. And another. Don't ever ride a freight train. It just isn't healthy, even though it might seem more convenient and faster than hitchhiking.

I'm proud to say that while I may have broken certain biblical commandments as well as one or two of my dad's, to this day I have never lost another pair of shoes, never ridden

48

a train unless I paid for passage, and I have never, *never*, asked a hobo where he's from.

New York hotel clerks ask guests signing in, "You wanna room for sleeping or for jumping?"

— Will Rogers, November 20, 1929

Chapter 5

"DON'T WASH 'EM SO CLEAN!"

I hadn't made much mileage during the night by riding the rods. The freight had been extremely slow, and I had paid little attention to the distance traveled. But by having only reached Gladewater, I had barely penetrated the huge Lone Star state.

The realization that I was, for the second time in my life, in Dad's native state brought a flood of memories to the surface. The first sojourn was a brief two years, 1920-21, when our family tried living in Beeville, in south Texas.

As I walked towards the main part of Gladewater, I wondered, as I had on previous occasions, why my father ever left this fabled land for the backwoods and swamps of Louisiana some time in the early part of this century.

I knew he had met Mother in and around the little towns of Kelly and Olla, in northeastern Louisiana, which were not far from where he worked at sawmills near the towns of Standard and Clarks. Though he first learned the carpenter's trade at Clarks, he finally ended up buying steers, which he then butchered to provide meat for mill employees.

Also, I had been told he was born near a place called

51

Brownsboro, in Henderson County, Texas. But I did not hear until many years later that his father was killed in a gunfight when Dad was still in diapers and that his mother had remarried quickly, as was usual in pioneering societies. She then moved with her new husband, named Killingsworth, to Prairie Dell, in Bell County. Near there, Dad attended his only school, for no more than a year or two.

His mother died before he was barely of school age. His stepfather soon remarried, so Dad lived with a stepfather and stepmother until his very early teens. There were also some half-siblings and step-siblings, the exact relationships a mystery to me at that time.

As I sauntered on alongside Hobo Fred toward a cluster of business buildings, other memories of Dad kept pace with our journey. I knew that he had left his step-home when he was thirteen or so, though he hadn't run away like me. He had simply, periodically, wandered off, doing odd jobs for nearby ranchers and friends until finally it was natural for him to stay away permanently.

It was during these years that he became adept at catching wild horses that still ranged the rolling hills of this mid-Texas country. He then rode and broke them into harness and saddle, and sold them. With this experience, he became what was called in those days a "hostler," later known as a "horse wrangler," one who knew horses and how to care for them.

I became more aware of our surroundings as we walked silently on into this booming oil town. Signs in store windows confirmed that we were indeed in Gladewater, Texas. This was evidently a new town, most of it anyway. There were no vacant stores or abandoned houses like the ones that dotted the scene in Louisiana. The Great Depression wave front must not have had Gladewater on its itinerary. Here was much new construction, with an atmosphere pervasive with the distinctive odor of recently sawn lumber intermingled with that of oil.

As we reached the center of town, in every direction, if a crude, newly erected building didn't obscure the view, a forest of oil derricks did — in front yards, side yards, back yards. In every open space there seemed to be an oil derrick in some stage of operation or development. Many were still drilling, with lights on, and there was a constant hubbub of roughnecks buzzing around under the commands of the tool pushers — the gang foremen.

It was an oil boom town all right — noisy, smelly and dirty, vibrating with energy — a very different environment from that prevailing in our depression-ravaged towns and cities.

Full daylight now greeted us as we walked down the unpaved main street, careful to avoid a never-ending stream of trucks, many hauling heavy oil well equipment of various kinds. It had rained recently — long enough ago for the muddy street to have partially dried, so that not much dust was kicked up by the heavy traffic.

Soon we noticed a cafe that was just opening up. To my amazement there was a sign in the window — "Dishwasher wanted" — without that usual limiting clause; "Only college graduates need apply."

Fred saw the object of my attention. He put his hand on my shoulder and said, "Go to it, son, and good luck," and walked on down the street without looking back.

I spoke to a man inside the cafe, "Sir, I'm applying for the dishwashing job."

He gave me a long, hard look. I squirmed in my "new" shoes, awaiting his reply.

"How old are you, son?" he asked gruffly.

"Seventeen, sir."

"Have your finished high school?"

"Yes, sir!" I blurted out and added hurriedly, "and I know how to wash dishes."

He still hesitated, "There's an awful lot of them, sonny." A short pause, then, "I'll give you a chance, if you can start right now. You'll get your meals, seventy-five cents a day, and a place to sleep."

Elated, I parked my bundle in an out-of-the way corner, rolled up my sleeves and prepared to step behind the counter.

"Hold on a minute, sonny. You'll need energy, and I suspect you haven't had breakfast, right?"

I nodded. He sat me on a counter stool and asked what I wanted. "Hot cakes!" I exclaimed. He put a short stack in front of me within what seemed like mere seconds, and before my bulging eyes added an egg, sunny side up, stating prophetically, "for the energy you're going to need,

53

sonny."

By the time I had finished my meal, patrons were pouring in. The cafe was narrow, barely large enough for the counter and ten stools with no tables. With all stools occupied, customers — men in soiled, stinking work clothes, obviously tired and with unshaven, unwashed faces — lined up behind the seats impatiently waiting their turn. The proprietor, with one assistant cook, had his hands full.

How I survived that morning rush, I do not now recall. We all were so busy that I rarely had a single word with the boss, other than a yell from him for "more dishes."

He had quickly introduced me to his dishwashing system first thing and apparently was going to let me sink or swim. To me, the system was a novel one. There was no such thing as running water, unless you count me running in and out the back door with a pail of water!

In the yard in back of the cafe was a washtub full of water heating over an open wood fire. I had to keep the fire going, dip a bucket into the tub and bring it in to the cafe, where I set it on a table too high for me to reach except from the top of a short, homemade footstool. At least one of my predecessors was as short as I!

My basic equipment consisted of two dishpans, one to wash in, the second for rinsing. The soap was a yellow bar, "store-boughten," I supposed, but it looked a lot like the old yellow lye soap my mother used to make years ago.

Even amid the hustle of the breakfast rush, the thought came to me: I sure wasn't "watering elephants" now but was still toting water — hot water in, dirty water out to be dumped into the thirsty backyard soil.

There was never a pause for rest, most of the morning. Every once in a while, I would feel the hand of the boss on my shoulder, as he reached in and picked up plates before I had finished rinsing and drying. He didn't say a word to me.

When the breakfast wave, supper for those who worked the graveyard shifts, was over, the boss took me aside and not unkindly said, "Sonny, I know you are new to this kind of arrangement, but you are going to have to speed it up — we need dishes for some hungry people, and I'm here to feed them."

All I could say was "Yes, sir." And I tried. I really

54

tried every way I knew how, to increase my production. But there were ingrained problems. I simply had to change the dirty water in both dishpans apparently more frequently than the boss would have, and I had to keep feeding wood to the fire to keep it alive. Once a day a water truck came along and left a barrel of water by the back door of the cafe. I used this to replenish the water heating over the fire.

I managed to get through lunch without the boss saying anything more, but I could sense him watching me out of the corner of his eyes. The lunch crowd was not as hectic as the breakfast one, so I managed to keep an adequate supply of clean dishes available most of the time.

In late afternoon, he directed me to a room in a house about a block away, off the main street, where I stored my bundle. He told me that this room was occupied in shifts, and that there would be no problem for me, since the other occupant worked during the night and only slept the early part of the day. Boomtowns have all kinds of shortages, I noted.

Dropping my bundle under the single bed, I returned to the cafe and tried to organize for the evening rush. Again I managed, despite a very busy couple of hours. About eight, the boss put seventy-five cents in my hands, steered me to a place where I could get a hot shower for twenty-five cents, and told me to get back by six the next morning.

Was the boss trying to tell me I needed a shower? I could only agree; I was long overdue. But the fact that a shower would cost one third of my cash earnings for one day bothered me. Water was a precious commodity in that boomtown where gasoline retailed at ten cents or less per gallon, but it was plain that the character of frontier life traditionally turns ordinary standards upside down and inside out.

I took his suggestion and paid my quarter for a fairly hot shower, although I had to put back on the same clothes I had previously been wearing. But after that shower I was probably as clean as anyone else in that boomtown, even more so than most.

My second day was no better than the first. I blamed my problem on the fact that Mother had taught me that a clean dish meant no food particles were left, visible or not.

55

Moreover, my science teachers had built into me a solid respect for germs. I had read about the early microbe hunters, especially a Dutchman named Leeuwenhoek who first spotted these invisible critters through his invention called a microscope.

Yet, after the boss had yelled his third plea for "More dishes! Hurry!" I began to question the standards I had been brought up with that now seemed to be working against me.

At the end of the day, while grabbing dishes out of my hands, the boss whispered savagely in my ear, "You don't have to wash 'em so clean! These men are hungry!"

I hadn't reached the age when I could come up with, a fast, logical rejoinder. My response should have been, "Why don't we buy more dishes?" though I doubt the suggestion would have set well coming from such a slow dishwasher. Besides, along with many other essentials, there probably was a shortage of dishes in this boomtown.

I slept soundly that night, even though I had skipped the costly hot shower. Two nights in a row seemed so unnecessary, if not indeed a luxury, on my income!

As the third day rolled around, there was no smile on the boss's face as he greeted me. But in spite of his cajoling and entreaties and demeanor, I still couldn't bring myself to hand him a dish with the yellow of an egg yolk staring back at me. Instinctively, I sensed he was peeved at my slowness.

Much sooner than usual, immediately after the lunch rush, he suggested I take an early afternoon nap. There was no reluctance on my part. I quickly made my way back to the rooming house. Paying no attention to my surroundings, in my fatigued state I undressed and crawled into bed, in the dimness of the room totally unaware that it already had an occupant.

The noise I made getting into the bed awakened him, and the next minute this huge animal of a man arose. I saw he was completely nude. Not only was he naked, he was falling-down drunk.

Alarm bells rang in my tired brain. I quietly reached under the bed where I had thrown my clothes and began to slip into them as he saw me more clearly and began wobbling in my direction. Next he held out his arms as if to embrace me.

I got out of there faster than out of any place before or since. And I managed to grab my bundle from under the bed as I did so. I'll never know what would have happened or whether he was so drunk he didn't know what he was doing, but I didn't hang around to find out.

As I hurried back to the cafe, I thought about the incident. Had I deliberately been sent to the room this early? Did the boss have this in mind to make it easier for him to fire me? Or for me to accept being fired?

I related to the boss what had happened, and was quite prepared for his answer: "Sonny, that's your room-mate, and I think it's best that you hit the trail, for your own good. I can't protect you from him."

He handed me fifty cents, said good-by and good luck, and out the door I went, fully believing that the real reason I had been let go was not because I'd been menaced by a drunken roommate but because I washed dishes too slow and too clean — at least, for Gladewater, Texas, when it was a booming oil town. To put it one way, it had been "germ warfare — and the germs had won!"

In my overall battle with the Great Depression, I would have to admit that Round Two was won by my antagonist, but not by a knockout. I was still standing. I refused to admit defeat as I slowly walked away from the downtown area.

"It takes hard writing to make easy reading."
— **Robert Louis Stevenson**

Chapter 6

"... HAVE SOME EXPERIENCES"

I didn't want to stay around Gladewater anymore. No doubt today it is a lovely city, hospitable to strangers, and I would feel better about it. But in 1932 the only place in town where I could feel comfortable was at or near the railroad, despite the scene I had witnessed there on my arrival. So I made my way there and, without too much difficulty, once more found a hobo jungle. This one was frequented by some younger travelers along with the usual older ones.

There was no common cookpot, as at the last hobo jungle I visited. Perhaps the half dozen hoboes lounging around were not hungry. But they were talking, which I found somewhat unusual.

Two of them were several years younger than I. They were buddies. The sound of their voices as well as their odd manner of speaking made me think they were Yankees, most likely from New York City.

Much of the conversation revolved around the merits of hitching rides on passenger trains. This was the fast way to get where one wanted to go, but also much more dangerous. Pros and cons on what was the best part of the train to

59

latch onto were discussed. There being no boxcars on passenger trains, one usually rode under a passenger coach on what was described as tie rods. Some hoboes argued that the safer, more comfortable place was in the narrow space between the baggage car and dining car.

Having no first-hand knowledge about the subject, I did not participate in the discussion. I had no intention of riding a passenger or even a freight train anymore, at least as a hobo. My only reason for being in this spot was that it was the only place I felt I wouldn't be unwelcome.

It was too late to start hitchhiking on the highway, and I thought I could somehow find a hole here for the night and start fresh in the morning. My next destination: Dallas.

It got a little more nippy as night approached, and finally someone started a fire. As a passenger train pulled out from the Gladewater depot, the two young kids and a third hobo hopped on it, right behind the baggage car, waved good-by and were gone.

I did my bit around the jungle by rounding up some firewood. As I was adding it to the blaze, one of the older men spoke up, "Son, did you get your newspaper?"

"No, sir, what do you mean?" I asked.

"To keep warm tonight. Looks like you didn't. Just so happens I've some extra here that I can spare," and he handed me a section from a Sunday paper. I thanked him, without clearly understanding why he thought I needed it. Before the night was over, I fully realized the value of what he had said. Newspaper can be very good to keep a body warm!

This was something I should have figured out on my own, for I had observed newspapers covering bare walls and holes of shacks in Louisiana occupied by poor blacks as well as whites. That included the bleak, unpainted tenant house we occupied in the "Colony" east of Monroe. The real purpose of this practice had not dawned on me until this moment, however. I even recalled the knotholes in the crude pinewood floors stuffed with paper in wintry weather, to stem the blasts of cold from the air spaces under these houses. Removing the paper made life more bearable during hot weather; fresh inserts prepared the structure for the next winter.

I observed how these older men curled up, usually

60

with their back to a log or tree or some solid object, and then spread newspaper over their bodies and laid a topcoat, or any other extra bit of apparel, over the paper. It made quite a distinctive, rustling sound as they shifted into position, but as slumber hit, the crackling of dry newspaper was duly submerged, to be replaced by the snores of deeply slumbering men. I followed suit as well as I could with the newspaper and found comfort in that layer of warmth in the early morning hours after the fire had completely died out.

Early the next morning I was first to stir. I betook myself quietly out of camp to nearby U. S. Highway 80 which led west to Dallas.

It was the beginning of autumn, with cool nights, but when the sun came out the days warmed up quickly. Before too long, I had left the wooded parts of east Texas and was traversing the more open plains, with fields of white bolls of cotton spread out as far as the eyes could see.

Though lucky to catch a series of rides that took me through this cotton-belt country, I was told time and again that if I was looking for work, I could earn anything from fifty cents to a dollar a day picking cotton.

Desperate as things were, I had not yet become discouraged enough to accept this well-meant advice. Cotton picking and I were not total strangers. I had picked and hoed cotton when I was just a tad, when Dad was a tenant farmer at a place called "The Colony," about ten miles due east of Monroe, Louisiana, where we had moved after Dad had given up the struggle in Beeville, Texas.

As on most small family farms, children helped out with chores of all kinds, especially when harvest time came around. Picking cotton was the hardest, it seemed to me, even more so than husking and shelling corn. Memories of backbreaking labor — through row after row plucking those white cotton bolls and tossing them into that heavy sack I dragged along — now flashed through my mind; these memories were too grim for me to even consider doing it again, especially since I was never really good at it. I was not yet that desperate.

I preferred a job jerking soda or washing dishes — at my pace, naturally. Besides, if I were to enter the cotton fields and were to "pick 'em too clean" I had real doubts that I could work fast enough to earn even fifty cents a day.

61

It took almost all day to cover the many miles to Dallas and I did a lot of walking between rides. The longest hitch, the one that took me near the center of Dallas, was provided by an unusual host—a "cereal-gun" salesman. He kept me enthralled with tales about the great invention he was peddling from city to city — a gun which converted whole grains into healthy breakfast cereals.

His prime targets were bread bakeries, which he predicted would each produce in the near future a local rival breakfast cereal and take much of the market away from the big, national guns at Kellogg's and at Post's, the storied makers of cornflakes and allied products.

The device he described to me as a large cannon was loaded with kernels of wheat or corn or other grains. A surge of electricity then exploded them into instant flakes of breakfast cereal which actually shot out into a bag receptacle.

For years afterwards I looked in vain for news of local breakfast cereals on sale in groceries. One more American dream that never got off the ground, I finally concluded. At least I was not the only unsuccessful dreamer! At that time I was unaware of "Quaker Oats — Shot from Guns" but doubt that this product had any connection with the device this itinerant cereal-gun salesman was promoting.

He dropped me off at a downtown corner in Dallas and gave me a good-luck wave which I returned. It was well after dark by the time I made my way to the public library, only to find it closed for the day. The library occupied a marble building that had huge columns on the front that reminded me of Southern colonial mansions.

Behind the column farthest from the doorway, I felt secure enough to drop my bundle and prepare for the night. After having a satisfactory meal bought with my meager fortune, I rescued a discarded newspaper from a nearby trash can and managed to cover my body with it. Then I topped it off with my half blanket. It was timely that I had learned this trick, as the night air piercing my summer duds was now chillier than ever.

The most precious items in my bundle were my "writings." Or so I imagined. The plan, now finalized in my mind in my fight with the Great Depression, was to present my best short story to an editor at the Dallas home office of *Hollands* and get started on the real career in my life — being a writer.

The morning sun awoke me as the city began to stir. I wandered the nearby streets as I waited for the library to open and spent more of my meager horde of coins, practically demolishing it, for a substantial breakfast. There were far more homeless people visible on the streets here than in Shreveport and Bossier City.

In front of one abandoned storefront was a line at least a half block long; everyone was waiting for a free meal at a mission. This was my first glimpse of this kind of charitable operation; I had not seen anything like it in Louisiana. As I passed by, I eyed the long, waiting line, and wondered if one day I would be reduced to standing in such a queue, which my upbringing taught was begging.

In this part of the city there were many vacant stores as well as other shabby, rundown buildings. I suspected that many of the hoboes I encountered on the street must have found a niche in some of them in which to spend the nights.

I returned to the library just as it was about to do business. As the massive doors swung open, I was first to enter. I headed straight for the map and newspaper section, where I thoroughly memorized the main routes in and out of Dallas in all directions and most importantly, the location of my goal: *Holland's: Magazine of the Southland*.

Holland's appeared to be many blocks east of the downtown area, so I decided to walk there in the late evening, after the library closed, and present myself to an editor early the next day. I spent the morning and early afternoon reading newspapers and going out for a good noon meal.

My library companions could have passed for the hoboes I had met on the road. Most of them used the reading room to catch up on their sleep. To accomplish this, they placed a newspaper vertically on a desktop and leaned over it with head bowed as if perusing it intently. Actually, they were supporting their heads on their arms, elbows resting on the table top.

I tried doing the same, but my arms weren't long enough. Besides, I was not as sleepy as so many of the others seemed to be.

After an hour or so in the warm room, the distinctive

odor of dirty clothes and unwashed bodies permeated the reading area. The smell didn't disturb me too much. After all, my brothers and I had worked for our dad in his abattoir. I was used to odors and scents of all kinds, and not the perfumed kind at that.

It was obvious that the library staff, however, didn't like the stuffy atmosphere. Ever so often one would exclaim, "You are not allowed to sleep in here. You will have to get out if you're not using the library properly."

I made it a point to use the library properly, studying every item in the daily papers, plus other periodicals available.

As evening approached, I took my belongings and myself for a long hike to *Holland's* headquarters — splurging on the way with my last coins to buy a hamburger, a glass of sweet milk and a piece of pie.

When I arrived in front of a multi-story building with *"Holland's, Magazine of the Southland"* emblazoned on it, I spied my night's lodging place: a vacant lot directly across the street. There were several large billboards on the lot, two of them making a ninety-degree angle at the corner of the lot. Behind the boards I discovered a hole about a foot deep and almost four feet long; it was probably dug by an animal, possibly a dog, but I welcomed it. It seemed tailor-made for my purposes.

The autumn winds now were definitely harbingers of winter, so I was thankful for the hole. Using ample newspaper, I managed to survive a much colder night than any I had experienced so far.

As morning arrived and signs of activity were visible at the front entrance of *Holland's,* I cleaned up my appearance as much as possible. I don't know how I must have looked to others, probably bedraggled and unkempt, but looks were not on my mind at the time. I was thinking only of seeing an editor and having my best-written product read.

I entered the lobby of the building feeling more confident than I had a right to and strode purposefully up to a receptionist's desk.

"I have some material for one of your editors to look over," I stated in as business-like a manner as I could muster.

The lady behind the desk appeared startled. She looked at me hesitantly for a few seconds and then picked up a phone and whispered something to the person on the other end. She then said, "Come with me. I'll take you to an editor."

I was thus ushered into the private office of a female editor. She said nothing other than "good morning," but her eyes examined me closely. I handed her my masterpiece, and waited.

She read it slowly. Then she looked at me across her desk as she handed the short story back and said, "Go out and have some experiences. Then come back with a story."

I had expected anything but this terse, cold statement; at least a question as to where I was from. Perhaps I had pictured a Miss Mary Thornton sitting across the desk from me, who would pucker the corner of her mouth and blow upward to move the wisp of hair from her eyes and then, in a gentle but positive voice, go over the good points of my scribbling before winding up with the bad features.

But this lady was not my beloved Mary Thornton. She was a practical, knowledgeable editor of one of my favorite periodicals. And her words burst my balloon of hope and dreams quickly, efficiently and lethally. So much so that it did not even occur to me that I should speak out that what I had handed her was written before I left home to become a hitchhiker, a boxer knocked out in a one-blow fight, an elephant water boy, and a boomtown cafe dishwasher fired for washing dishes too clean! All in the short time of a few, brief weeks. Would it have made any difference?

I said nothing as I picked up my manuscript and left, but I was devastated.

Since I was only seventeen and had worked only since I was twelve, I didn't have enough savvy to do the logical thing and ask that efficient lady editor for some other kind of job, such as, an errand boy, someone to sweep up, someone in the mail room. Does such hindsight plague other people too, I later wondered?

Slowly, dejectedly, I headed back downtown in the general direction of the library. In fact, I took most of the day getting there, in a numbed state of mind, unable to focus on my next move. I do not remember what I saw or did during that day's wandering toward the main business district, and then around it countless times.

Mostly I merely ambled slowly along in a daze, unable to think clearly about anything.

Near sundown, I found myself in my corner behind the library column where I could half doze and look at the want ads in a morning paper salvaged from a trash basket. At the moment, my mind was a complete blank on my next move — in fact, for the first time there was no foreseeable next move.

As the curtain of darkness descended on this crushing day, I made my nest and tried to sleep, although that empty feeling of returning hunger pains began to assail me.

Tomorrow, I thought, tomorrow after a good night's sleep is a better time to analyze the situation. Then I'll be able to determine what my next step will be.

One thing I knew for certain. I would not give up my quest and head home. I refused to even think about calling it quits. The Great Depression had knocked me down in this Round Three, but not out. It hadn't beaten me yet, and never would.

Bolton High in Alexandria, Louisiana, where the author's beloved Miss Mary Thornton served as faculty advisor of the **Cumtux**, *the school paper.*

"In its majestic equality, the law forbids rich as well as poor from sleeping in doorways, begging in streets — and stealing bread."

— W. Jay Morgan

Chapter 7

ORANGE PEEL BRUNCH

As the Great Depression continued, in many places one out of three employables was jobless. That percentage soared even higher elsewhere. Thousands of homeless men, some with wives and children, roamed the U.S., hitchhiking or riding the rails from city to city, town to town, some from east to west, others west to east, from north to south in wintry days, south to north in warm ones, in fruitless efforts to find work or food or both.

Few were professional hoboes, though I have used the "hobo" as a generic term for all the homeless that I met. Most were grown men looking to help their families back home, but an increasing number of the young and very young overflowed the main routes and larger cities in the summer, fall and winter of 1932. Most still retained at least a faint hope of finding a solution to their problems, though the number of faces that reflected utter despair was mounting.

Homegrown food was still ample on farms and ranches in many areas, while in cities more and more families went on starvation or near-starvation rations. How could there be such hunger in our great land of plenty? Here's how: the foodgrowers found it too costly to harvest and ship to places where demand existed, even while food rotted on the ground and became slop for pigs and hogs — which, in turn, could not be economically moved to markets and sold even if would-be customers had the necessary money.

Those businesses that survived did so mainly by trimming every possible cost, including reduced wages for long-time employees and dismissing nonessential, newer workers, often with no advance notice. Family-run and small enterprises managed to hang on by working long hours and cutting all corners. The famed apple or pencil sellers, with stands on busy street corners, no doubt existed in the largest cities, but I never encountered them in my journey probably because I avoided the busiest street corners where their best prospects for sales were to be found.

Amidst this climate of despair the campaign for the election of our national president was underway. From the state of New York, candidate Franklin Delano Roosevelt was claiming that as a fellow farmer he fully understood the problems facing the many struggling tillers of the soil, and he promised he would do something about it when elected. He made other promises to the rest of America, but that particular one struck me most forcefully as I sat in the Dallas Public Library scanning the daily papers.

I spent another night in the corner behind my favorite column and, as now seemed natural, awoke hungry the next morning, a Friday. I left the library and took to the streets to search for work of any kind. I made the rounds again, but restaurant jobs were unavailable, even for college graduates, nor were soda jerk applicants in demand.

The streets of Dallas, especially downtown near the central library, teemed with ragged, scruffy men and boys of all ages. Some, like me, had not reached the point of utter hopelessness and were obviously looking for work. Others, clearly in a state of despair with no prospects of finding work, were just marking time, striving to stay alive while waiting for who knows what to happen who knows when.

I dawdled most of that day, still in a daze from my

bitter disappointment at *Holland's*. When I looked back on it afterward, I realized that this was the lowest point of my life. Though I had disappointments later, I was always able to select the next target and move toward it with some hope of success. But, on this day, in an increasingly cold Dallas, I was unable to decide on my next step.

Finally, in late afternoon I managed to pull myself together enough to meander aimlessly around the streets. More by accident than intent I wandered into a shabbier part of the downtown area, composed of secondhand stores of all kinds, including as well a number of rundown pawnshops.

Gnawing hunger pains finally gave me courage enough to timidly enter one of the shoddiest-looking pawnshops. A white-haired lady asked my desires, and without previous planning or much thinking, I held out the only possession I could part with, a well-worn wallet that had seen its last days months before.

"I'd like to pawn this for some money, please."

The lady slowly took the wallet from my outstretched hand, looked at it disparagingly, started to return it but paused as she gave me a closer inspection.

"When was your last meal?" she inquired.

"Two days ago, ma'am."

She motioned, "Come with me."

She took my arm and with some reluctance I let her lead me into a back room which turned out to be a combination kitchen-dining area. She sat me at the small table, went to the stove, and from a pot heating on its top dipped out a bowlful of black-eyed peas with a piece of fat floating on the surface.

"Eat it!" she commanded in a stern but motherly tone of voice.

Eat it I did, and eagerly, though embarrassed at first to open my mouth. When through, I mumbled my thanks as well as I could, and as I passed this kind lady on the way out she pressed a nickel into my left hand, though she kept the wallet. No doubt it ended up in the trashcan the moment I exited through the front door.

Refreshed, and in a numbed state of mind not feeling at all guilty about my pawnshop visit, I ambled back by a different route to the library, testing the employment situa-

69

tion along the way. Not a nibble did I get.

With no bath since Gladewater, and keeping my clothes on twenty-four hours a day, there was no doubt my appearance was really grubby and tattered. I can now understand why I got short shrift at most of the places I entered.

Once again, back in the library, I buried my face in another Dallas newspaper, reading it from front to back, then back to front — just to kill time until bedtime.

After another night in my usual spot, with the temperature dipping still lower than the night before, I was again first into the library when it opened. The day before, I had read an article that now, finally, began to penetrate my still sluggish mind and brought me back to life enough to do some thinking.

It was an article about Brazil, in South America. It said the Brazilians were holding out a welcoming hand to Americans who wished to emigrate. But now that I reread it, I noticed that it was farmers they wanted, and though born on a farm I surely was far removed from being a farmer.

Sometime or other I had also seen an item about the Matanuska Valley settlement in Alaska looking for immigrants to farm there. Could anyone use someone other than farmers, I asked myself? Cold Alaska did not entice me. I didn't like the visions of ice and snow that place evoked. It brought back memories of the winter of 1922-23 when we lived in a small town called Swartz, twelve miles northeast of Monroe, in the northeast corner of Louisiana.

Swartz — that was where I had enrolled in the first grade of grammar school. (Most of the Louisiana that I knew didn't know what kindergarten was in those days.) This was another boomtown, of gas, not oil. The town's sole industry at that time was a processing plant turning natural gas into carbon black to be used in manufacturing many commercial products.

Being a boomtown, there were not enough houses for all the workers, and Dad was employed there as a carpenter to help build more. He got the job during the winter when we lived on the farm in "The Colony." He had to trek five miles in the dark through a swamp and dense woods to and from his work. And his ten to twelve hour day earned him the excellent wage of five dollars per day.

70

I remembered the miner's cap and lantern he bought in order to follow the dim path through the swamp, until eventually we were able to move to Swartz. We sometimes feasted on possum or squirrel that he shot on the way home at night. Possum and sweet potatoes! Is it normal for extreme hunger to trigger memories of special treats?

Because of the housing shortage, our whole family lived in two tents when we moved to Swartz — a large wall tent which housed our parents and sister, with a smaller tent we called the "caboose" in back for my two brothers and me. And that was one of the coldest winters on record in northeast Louisiana. Not only did it snow, it sleeted! Even the mill pond between our tents and the schoolhouse was completely iced over, and the sleet on the ground seemed to be extremely deep and slippery, producing a numbing cold.

As I sat in the Dallas Library that October 1932 day, with my elbows on the table barely holding up the newspaper in front of me, I continued to read news accounts of warmer places. It seemed to me that Brazil could be my cup of tea. It had to be a toasty warm place. But it was such a long way off. To get to it, I had to go through a city I had heard about ever since I was five, San Antonio, Texas.

In 1920 and 1921 my family had lived in Beeville, about 100 miles south of San Antonio. In the warmth of the Dallas library, I began to daydream of those milder days in Beeville. I recalled it was there that I encountered my first newspaper comic strips.

They came on the railroad each Saturday from the big city up north. It was the Sunday editions of the San Antonio newspapers that introduced me to the thrilling adventures of Andy and Chester Gump, Bringing up Father (Maggie and Jiggs), Little Orphan Annie and Daddy Warbucks, the Katzenjammer Kids, and others who stayed around a long, long time, a lifetime for many of us.

Whatever Dad was doing in Beeville, or trying to do, failed. Consequently, we had some lean days toward the end. One meal stands out in particular — my favorite breakfast of cornflakes, not with milk poured over it, but with water! I ate it and thus escaped the pangs of hunger — until now that is, in the Great Depression.

But Beeville had never been as cold as this Dallas. Perhaps San Antonio would not be either. Thus, while my future plans were beginning to ferment, my stomach growled a warning that I had better spend my last nickel, my profit from the pawnshop deal!

So I hit the streets again, looking for a five-cent hamburger for lunch, and found one.

I also observed more closely the long line of men, and boys my age and even younger, standing silently in front of the store that had been converted into a soup kitchen. On closer inspection I noted it was operated by some kind of religious organization. The sign out front stated: "Pray and sing with us — and get a free meal."

I spotted a platform inside where a preacher was just opening up a Bible on a podium. I was not yet desperately hungry enough to attend a sermon to earn a meal, so back to the library I scurried.

On Saturday, Dallas was not nearly as crowded as on a normal business day, at least not in this section of downtown. Directly opposite the library entrance was a parking lot. This Saturday it was only partially filled with customers, and for a moment I toyed with the idea of going up to the man in charge to ask about a job parking cars. (Customers didn't park their own, as they do now in most places.)

But I really didn't know all I should about driving cars, especially those with the newfangled gear shifts. I had learned to drive my father's model-T truck, with the hand crank and the gas and spark levers on the steering wheel. I did not dare get behind the steering wheel of one of the more modern vehicles like those I had seen in the lot.

I spent the remainder of the day inside the library until I was ejected at closing time.

I went to bed early that evening, my head now more alert and churning with ideas and plans about what I should do. I had not yet reached a decision about where to head next or what to do, but it seemed as if a decision were close. I just needed a key word, a trigger to bring it to consciousness.

As I wriggled into the most comfortable position possible on the concrete nest behind my column, it seemed that the night air was now colder, almost frigid. I spent an almost sleepless night, tossing and turning and contorting my body. Near dawn, when it is usually coldest, I curled up in a tight ball inside my newspaper-blanket cocoon to keep all body heat close to me.

72

As soon as the morning sun warmed things somewhat, I sat up with my back to the library wall. With the library closed on Sunday, I had nowhere to go, so I sat and daydreamed and looked at the empty parking lot across the street. But, lo! It was not entirely empty; clearly visible near the cashier's booth I spotted something orange-looking, lying on the concrete.

As the day wore on, my curiosity got the better of me. Somehow I gathered the energy to pull myself erect and amble over to inspect the object. It was the remnants of an orange peel with a few particles of flesh still clinging to the skin.

I stared at it longingly. The picture of a complete orange loomed in my imagination, tantalizing me.

I fought the urge to reach down, pick up the peel and swallow it. After another day without food, I am not sure I would have hesitated. But I controlled the feeling and retreated slowly to my corner of the library entrance, not quite yet a complete savage.

The niche was pleasantly warm as long as the sun's rays hit that side of the building. So I stayed there all morning and into the afternoon, knowing most enterprises closed on Sundays. Then, to my surprise, a few cars entered the lot and parked. There was no barrier to keep them from parking free on this day.

Why couldn't I walk over and tell a driver I would keep an eye on his car for a nickel? I actually considered it. If I had regained my self-confidence by that time, I believe I could have put action into the idea. But a glance at my dirty, smelly clothes killed any thought of talking with another human being about a job.

I remembered the impulse many times in later years' visits to Mexico, where I was besieged by kids younger than I had been, who offered to guard my car for a peso. They were actually doing what I was too timid to try on this Dallas Sunday afternoon in 1932.

Near the end of the day as the rays of the sun shifted from my corner, it was necessary to move around to keep warm. I figured it would be smart to find some extra newspaper if I were to endure the coming night. Walking slowly toward a nearby street corner where a trash can stood, I saw people waiting on the corner for buses. I probably looked to them like a filthy homeless waif, which I must admit I was.

One of the men stared at me so intensely as I rummaged through the trash can, that I became nervous. Finally he walked over and asked me where I was from, if I was looking for work, and so on. Since no hobo would have asked such questions, he clearly was not one, so I briefly answered him.

Just then his bus drew up to the curb. As he turned to board it, he pressed a dime in my hands and, obviously embarrassed, said, "Get something to eat," and was gone before I could recover from my surprise and find a word to say. Thus I had a dime in my hand and could now afford a bite for that void called a stomach.

"Was this panhandling?" I asked myself — something that would have shamed my dad if he knew. No, it wasn't. I hadn't asked the man for money. He had simply thrust it upon me. But I did not feel happy about it. A small voice that was the echo of my father's teaching reminded me that a good person always works for his money. And I surely hadn't earned this dime.

This memory of Dad's maxim did not deter me from finding a place that sold a ten-cent bowl of chili, which warmed me enough to face my nook for another cold night, protected with added layers of insulating newspapers salvaged from trash cans.

Monday was a repeat of my daily pattern of life, if one could call this living. First into the library to get out of the cold of early October and to read the morning newspaper thoroughly until the sun had warmed up outside. A fruitless survey of job possibilities, followed at noon by a closer inspection of the long soup line outside the mission.

As evening approached, my stomach again took control of my morals and my upbringing. Or can one say that it is work to listen to a sermon in order to get a free meal? Hunger can say a lot of strange things, I had discovered. By now hunger told me it would be okay to hear what the minister had to say, before sitting down to a hot "free" meal.

At last I surrendered, joined the soup line, and then took my place in a pew to hear half an hour of hell and damnation from a fundamentalist preacher. The sermon did not spoil my appetite. I feasted on a balanced meal for the first time in the great city of Dallas.

Then, back to my library hideaway for another night, covered by layers and layers of newspapers. I had to make a decision about my next move soon I realized, as I spent another night trying to keep warm and get some shut-eye also.

The next morning, as I entered my library headquarters, for the first time I left my bundle in what I had now begun to think of as my special haven. It was well-concealed from casual passersby. I was afraid that my shabby possessions coupled with body odor would provide an excuse for the library staff to eject me as I had seen them do another homeless critter the day before.

I mulled all morning over what I should do next in my quest. At noontime, when sunlight had warmed things up outside, I returned to pick up my bundle from its secret place. It was gone! My stolen shoes episode had not taught me enough, it appeared. My secluded shelter obviously had not been a secret to somebody who had a greater need than I for at least my half blanket. But the thief had also taken everything else, including my precious manuscripts!

The incident raised my ire. Filled with anger I circled the block, looking in every trash and garbage can and pail that might contain some of my cherished possessions. But no luck.

At the end of the search, standing morosely on the street as wintry winds began to whistle around the corner, I finally knew what to do next. Go south! Go to where it is warmer.

This theft of everything I owned except the clothes on my back provided the elusive key I had been searching for. The days of indecision and wavering and doubting were over. Intermission was over and I was ready for the next round in my battle with the Great Depression. I shifted into high gear and headed toward the highway, going south without looking back at Dallas where I had almost received a knockout blow from the Great Depression.

My plan was to stop first in San Antonio. Depending on events there, then perhaps on to Brazil? Who knows? At least I was doing something about the situation. And as the cold winds pierced my thin garments, I was pleased to be headed to where it was warmer.

75

"It's always darkest before the dawn."

— **Winston Churchill**

Chapter 8

EL CAMINO DEL VAGABUNDO

The first highway in Texas not of Indian or animal origin started out as a trail in the days of the earliest Spanish expeditions into the wilderness. As more and more adventurous souls traveled it, it became known as El Camino Real, the Royal Road or King's Highway.

Remnants of this ancient road still exist. Starting in Mexico it moves through *San Antonio de Bexar* from whence it traverses the state in an easterly by northerly direction. It then crosses into Louisiana on the boundary east of Nacogdoches, Texas, and west of Natchitoches, Louisiana.

When Texas was part of Spain and later of Mexico, many immigrants made their laborious way on this old road to get to San Antonio, the only pueblo of any size in the early days, and the largest city in the state until the 1900s when Dallas and then Houston pushed it down to third place.

My journey to San Antonio did not take me on that historical Royal Road. I have described it to contrast the "unroyal" road I followed. My route from Dallas to San Antonio in 1932 could more aptly be called "El Camino del Vagabundo" — Highway of the Tramp. In the Great Depression (and even today) many homeless roamed this highway, trying to reach warmer climes as well as kinder hearts and better prospects.

The Spaniards apparently did not subdivide the "homeless," as Americans do, into tramps and hoboes. While English dictionaries may make little distinction between the two terms, in my experience a hobo is a homeless person willing to work for his or her food while a tramp is on a lower scale, along with "beggar," one who begs for sustenance with no actual desire to work. I considered myself a hobo, not a tramp — despite the gift a few days earlier of the dime from that sympathetic Dallasite. He had been as embarrassed to give as I had been to get, though my hunger in the end had won out.

As I headed south from Dallas on this Camino del Vagabundo one day in October 1932, I looked forward to finding warmer weather in San Antonio, or to traveling farther south if I had to in order to uncover a job opportunity. Nor was Brazil yet ruled out as a last-ditch destination.

Down to the clothes on my back, with the cold breath of approaching winter breathing down my neck, I was inspired to a more fervent effort for a hitch, a ride. Besides, there was now more competition along the roadside, as many other hoboes had also felt the chill of those icy gusts and were equally intent on thumbing their way to a warmer clime.

Daylight was ending as I reached a city whose name had always fascinated me: Waco. As a soda jerker in the Owl Pharmacy, I had used the word "Waco" on many occasions as a sodajerker's code name for Dr. Pepper, reputed to have originated in Waco, Texas. (A code word for Coca-Cola was "shoot one" or "dope." For some reason, the slang for a glass of water was "81," for two glasses, "82," and so on. In Pineville and Central Louisiana, we also had our own unique concoction called a "jellybean" soda, code for a cherry nectar. This milk drink was enabled to retain its cherry flavor by diluting the strong cherry syrup with the correct proportion of "simple," i.e. plain, syrup, so the milk and cherry mixture would not curdle.)

Most of those who gave me a lift were small-town salesmen, none going very far. But usually the ones who picked me up were alone, wanted company and enjoyed talking, mostly about their business or sad lack of it. Rarely was I questioned too closely about mine.

I had abandoned my tale of visiting a relative in Fort Worth, as that city lay in a different direction. Now I frankly stated that I was looking for work so I could send money back home to the family. After all, the highway was filled with thumb-waving homeless people like me, some younger, most older, all headed for better weather and most looking for jobs.

I did not get to stop in Waco, for I was lucky enough to get a lift through it and the city of Belton some miles beyond. Just south of Belton, a genial farmer-rancher gave me my last, short ride of the day, letting me off near the entrance to his place. I did not know exactly where this was, but I thanked the man for his kindness and started walking on down the roadway. It was now twilight, and I was keenly aware that somehow I had better find shelter against the blowing north winds that were beginning to whip up more strongly.

I noticed the dim outline of a large, unpainted barn on the east side of the highway. A coal-oil lamp in the nearby house suddenly flickered into light. Cold, hungry, and filthy, I figured I was in no condition to go up to the dwelling and ask to do some work in exchange for a night's food and lodging. Instead, keeping the structure between me and the house, I cautiously opened the barn door facing the road. In the dimness inside I discerned hay spilling over from a loft.

I was in luck. There were no farm animals to become disturbed by my presence. I quickly went up a ladder and across a sea of yielding hay to the farthest corner, dug a nice deep depression, crawled into it and pulled handfuls of hay over my body and head. Slumber followed quickly. That was one of the coziest beds I have ever slept in.

(Years later, a South Texas friend assured me that poisonous snakes also find hay in barns a snug place to winter. Even if I had known that then, on such a cold night I do not believe it would have influenced my decision to shelter there.)

The first light of day — false dawn actually — greeted my eyes. Wide awake and still hungry, I moved carefully, but with alacrity, to leave the scene before my unwitting host visited the barn. I made it out to the highway and walked briskly southward to ward off the morning chill.

In the dim pre-dawn light, I shortly passed a tiny cluster of wooden frame buildings in a small business community. On one such building I made out the first word on a weather-beaten sign: "Prairie..." The remaining word was too faint for me to decipher.

Years later I discovered that the barn in which I had spent a night on El Camino del Vagabundo was owned by a man named Killingsworth, a younger stepbrother of my father, and that the small community was Prairie Dell, Bell County, where my father moved with his mother and stepfather, J. H. Killingsworth, about 1876, and lived until he wandered away at age 13 or 14 to make his own way in life. Up to this point in my peregrinations, he had succeeded far better than I.

Most of us have moments when we dream "what if ...," a game played usually after we become adults. Like most adults sometimes I have conjectured what course my life might have taken had I knocked on the door of Mr. Killingsworth's home before I trespassed into his barn.

In my ignorance of the significance of this location, and in a hurry to get to a warmer place, I continued on, aided by my now well-educated thumb. But rides were few and far between on this day. Those who did stop for me were usually traveling only short distances.

Thus it was late afternoon before I arrived in Austin, the state capital, just some 90 miles by those older winding roads from my next goal, San Antonio.

Making my way to Austin's city library, I studied the maps so I would know the best route to take south the next morning. Hunger, and a little experience, now drove me to ask the librarian where there might be a soup kitchen available. I was beginning to learn a valuable lesson: that sooner or later in everyone's life, one must — or should — ask for help.

I was directed to a soup kitchen not too far away, and I was thankful I did not have to listen to a sermon before a heaping plate of beans and beef was placed before me. I stuffed myself. Like the original pioneers into this storied state, I thought, "Feast today; famine the next three!"

The soup kitchen also had dormitories for itinerants such as myself. Fortunately we were not yet nearly as

80

numerous as in Dallas, so beds were available. After I had eaten as much as I could, I went to the man in charge of the sleeping accommodations. Again, kindness intervened to save me from having to take a cot in the middle of a crowd of smelly, snoring adults.

The manager took one look at me and said, "I usually don't let anyone sleep in my room, but I have an extra cot there that you can use. You look like you need some real rest, and you're not as dirty as these bums." Maybe I wasn't as dirty as those bums, but by now even I could hardly stand my own odor. I hadn't had a bath since Gladewater, many days ago!

I asked if I could shower, and the manager showed me where to go. I took my time removing all the grime and dirt I could find. Drying was a problem, since I didn't have a towel, but I let the air dry me before I went to my cot and slipped under a fresh sheet and blanket. Still a little damp, I worried that I would not leave the cot as clean as I found it.

This turned out to be true in a different and embarrassing way, as the beans and my abused stomach were not as compatible as they should have been. I found myself running to the bathroom at odd hours of the night, sometimes just a little too late to avoid a minor accident. Ashamed of having dirtied the manager's fresh sheet, I arose before anyone else and by first light was on my way out of the downtown area and back onto El Camino del Vagabundo headed toward San Antonio.

Again, rides were relatively short ones. It took almost all day to go the 90 miles from Austin to San Antonio. As usual, I headed straight for the public library which was on the banks of the San Antonio River. This library was considerably smaller than the one in Dallas and did not have huge columns at the front. My sleeping arrangements would be different here, I realized. But at least the weather seemed a good deal friendlier.

The library was overcrowded with fellow vagabonds, so I escaped to wander around and look over the outside situation. With darkness coming on, I grabbed used newspapers from a *brazura*, Spanish for a trash container, and carried them with me as I walked across the river and up Alamo Street to Alamo Plaza.

Here stood the revered Alamo, the old Catholic

mission that became the rallying symbol of Texans in their battle with Mexico for freedom. South of the Alamo grounds stands the famous Menger Hotel, built a few years after the fall of the Alamo, which coats it with a patina of ageless respectability. Among other famous guests, Teddy Roosevelt had made it his headquarters when he recruited and trained the Rough Riders for our war with Spain in 1898.

In the middle of Alamo Plaza this October day, 1932, almost directly opposite the entrance to the Menger Hotel, stood a bandstand and a public toilet — both long since torn down. There were shade trees and benches all around, so the Plaza seemed a perfect spot to make my bed for my first night in San Antonio.

It was not meant to be. I had picked out a secluded, unoccupied bench, all right, and had just finished cocooning my body with newspapers and was closing my eyes to doze off when I felt a tap on my shoulder.

I looked up into the face of a man in uniform, a policeman. Not an auspicious start for Round Four with the Great Depression! In alarm I sat up.

"Son," he said kindly, "you can't sleep here. Let me tell you what to do."

He then directed me due west, back along Market Street past the library, several more blocks west to a plaza where the county courthouse was situated. Cater-cornered from the courthouse was the combined police station and city jail.

I went down into the basement where a huge furnace roared a welcome. Its warmth permeated the entire area. Next to it, stretched out on newspapers, another hobo was already slumbering soundly. I laid my paper pallet next to his, and was soon just as asleep. My last thought as I drifted into slumberland was, "What a friendly town this is!"

And so, thanks to the kindness of the "Alamo" City Police Department, I spent my first night in San Antonio in its jail.

How would the rest of Round Four go?

82

"Success: get up one more time than you're knocked down!"

—Peter Principle edited by Jay Morgan

Chapter 9

CALICHE LAUNDROMAT

While hoboes were not as numerous in San Antonio, they were a good deal friendlier. Was it because of the warming rays of the sun? Or because of the natural warmth emanating from the natives of this hospitable city?

Anyhow, when my sleeping neighbor woke up, he broke hobo rules and made friends with me in the jailhouse basement. Though younger than I, he had been on the road a lot longer and was wiser in the ways of the hobo world.

When he found out I had arrived only the afternoon before, he volunteered to lead me to the "breakfast place," which turned out to be a food line on South Alamo Street, in an old Spanish-style adobe building. I never found out who the generous host or organization was, but hot oatmeal and buttered toast, along with a steaming cup of weak (to one raised in Louisiana) Texas-style coffee, tuned up my insides. Besides, there was no preaching to listen to before the food was doled out!

While there was no sermon, the men and boys in this long waiting line were not silent. Warmth and friendliness had loosened tongues, for they were making statements that

I would never forget. The campaign for President of the United States was well underway by this time, and the candidates were undergoing the verbal scrutiny of these hoboes. Away from their homes, they had no votes, but they certainly had voices.

These were not all illiterate bums but men down on their luck due to the Depression. Many were obviously educated beyond the high school level. They said, "If we don't get some help from the government, it'll be time for a revolution," and "If the government can't help, it's time for a dictator, like that guy Hitler in Germany."

This kind of talk I heard over and over from men who walked the streets daily in a search for any kind of employment.

There were also comments like "Brazil wants Americans to live there. They say there's a future with them, certainly enough for a body not to starve."

"Yeah, but how you gonna get to Brazil? That's a helluva lotta miles from here."

Some talk was upbeat about a presidential campaign promise to revoke the Prohibition Amendment that forbade the sale of liquors and beer. The majority were in favor of this, as it would create many new jobs — and, of course, that was what this group was interested in the most.

Others reported that they had observed fruit lying rotten on the ground and trees overloaded with fruit which the owners could not afford to pick and ship to the markets. In other areas, they said, the same situation existed with vegetables. The only advantage to the owners of having such produce was that they could eat it themselves. They starved less frequently than city dwellers — at least until "northers," cold winds blowing out of the northwest, later blasted layers of dust off farms and ranches in Oklahoma and elsewhere in the Great Plains states.

The craziness of going hungry in a land of plenty, with no way to bring necessities to the needy, was all too apparent to these men waiting for a breakfast handout.

Overhearing it all, I firmly resolved to sharpen my wits and attack the Great Depression with more vigor in this round. I made up my mind that I would explore completely all job possibilities in San Antonio before throwing in the towel and heading south to Brazil. I hoped never again to have someone throw in a white towel for me. I certainly didn't wish to do it to myself.

With the renewed energy and optimism the Spartan but warming breakfast generated, I determined my best shot was to get better acquainted with the city before testing its job market. So I set out to explore the lay of the land and the charming San Antonio River more fully.

First-time visitors to the Alamo city often belittle the river that flows through it and say it's only a creek or small stream, pointing out that it's no wider than a narrow street. Nevertheless it is a grown-up river — and has proven it many times at flood season.

It has an unusual shape in downtown San Antonio. From its origin just north of Brackenridge Park, the main channel flows south, past the courthouse, but just beyond Houston Street another channel branches off and winds eastward several blocks, then swings south three or four blocks. It then turns westward and flows behind the old library building (now housing the Hertzberg Circus Museum) on Market Street, to rejoin the main channel a little south of a line with the front of the courthouse. In other words, the river makes this part of the entire downtown core an island, though most people are unaware of it.

Sadly, on this October day in 1932, the Great Depression scourge was clearly evident. Seemingly half of the buildings on this island were boarded up and vacant. Others displayed "Going out of Business" signs.

I traced the entire bank of the island and then headed south a few blocks beyond the courthouse area to what was the first exclusive residential section of old San Antonio, known as the King William district.

Stately homes on wonderfully wide streets laid out in straight rows, bordered with tall spreading oak and pecan trees, constituted a novelty in this part of Texas. Here many of the first German immigrants who succeeded in the earliest business enterprises built their mansions adjacent to the winding San Antonio River and sent their children to the first public school, taught in German. They probably used river water for many purposes at first, until wells were dug which in turn were supplanted by the public water system.

I walked slowly past these old homes with their beautiful, manicured lawns and shaded yards, sensing a mood of success, peace and contentment. Across the river, on the west side, I could see a stone tower several stories high. The words "Pioneer Flour Mill" were clearly displayed on it.

About a block or so south of the King William section and the Pioneer Flour Mill, I descended the steep banks and walked beside the crystal-clear waters of the river until I reached a spot around a bend concealed from view by foliage and bushes. The curve was situated just right for warding off any chilling winds from the north, while capturing the full, warming rays of the sun.

Here I took off all my clothes, including my shorts, appropriated some of the clay, termed *caliche* by the natives, that lined the bank, and began to pound and briskly rub my clothes with chunks of the stuff. Having read in *National Geographic* about women in a foreign country laundering their clothes somewhat in this fashion, I deemed it worth the effort to rid myself of the embarrassing odors that accompanied me.

I literally spent hours at this spot, working over every thin garment I had left, tackling every soiled spot I could see, and then dipping the garment in the cold, flowing waters of the river until all traces of the cleansing clay had vanished. As each garment seemed clean, at least cleaner and less smelly than before, I hung it on a branch to catch the sunshine.

By midafternoon I was through, my clothes were dry and back in place. I felt refreshed, though a little hungry, of course, but more confident than I had been for days — since before my visit to *Holland's,* as a matter of fact. My welcome in this old Spanish town had imbued me with more than a faint glimmer of hope.

I walked up onto the bank and along the wide streets of this exclusive King William neighborhood. As I sauntered along, drinking in the peaceful, quiet beauty of the area, I recalled overhearing some of the hoboes talk about signs and symbols secretly placed by tramps over the back doors or entrances to houses, to indicate whether it was a place to be avoided, or whether the right approach could result in a free meal. I didn't know what these symbols were, and never wanted to, as I intended to live by Dad's rule of honest work for honest pay.

86

But hunger pains still ruled the day, so I paused in front of one house which looked warm and hospitable and possibly of the type that would exchange some food for some yard work. I made up my mind, then went around to the back of the house and knocked hesitantly on the door.

A large Hispanic lady answered. "Yes, what ees it?"

"I'm looking for work, ma'am, yard work, anything around the house — or even in the house?"

She paused before replying, took a good hard look at my newly scrubbed clothes, even sniffed a little. "We don' need work. If you hungry, you come in."

I came in. Pinto beans, Mexican style. I'll always love them.

As I left, I thanked the lady, who must have been the cook for the owner. She made a motion with her left hand as she opened the back door with her right, and said, "Vaya con Dios, young man. Go with God!"

I thanked her again, with my high school Spanish this time. As I walked away, I stuck my hands in my pocket and discovered a thin dime that had not been present before. That lady must have sneaked it there when she bid me farewell.

My feeling of warmth towards this friendly city was reinforced. And the thought came to me that the kindly cook must have felt rewarded by making this small gift to a hungry youth. That thought was sufficient to deter me from going back to return the gift.

Back to the library again to peruse the newspapers for anything that looked like a job for a teenager trying to survive long enough to grow up.

The reading area was suffocating with the odor of hoboes and tramps, much more noticeable now that I had cleaned up, so much so that a librarian soon opened windows to let in a draft of fresh air.

I read the want ads very carefully in both the *Express* morning and the *Light* afternoon papers, but was unable to spot anything that looked inviting. I decided to explore more of the city, to get a better feel of it. I was definitely falling under the magic spell of its warmth and charm.

Off I went, westward still, to the older section of downtown, heavily populated with Mexican-Americans, almost all of whom were native-born Texans, though not all

87

spoke English. Walking through the streets and barrios, I observed the many individual small businesses that were surviving even in this Great Depression.

Many consisted of pushcarts peddling hot tamales or slices of pumpkin and sweet potatoes glazed with sugar. Many small shops also existed, where I saw fat Mexican ladies grinding corn on their stone metates, mixing it with water, kneading this masa, and then flipping the flattened *tortilla*, a unique symbol of Mexico, onto a hot plate over a wood fire, until it was done.

As suppertime approached, my dime began burning a hole in my pocket. I stopped in front of one such tortilla stand and asked the price of a tortilla. A nickel, half my fortune, would buy six warm tortillas! I then halted at a pushcart and handed over the other half of my fortune for a large piece of pumpkin, coated with a sugar glaze. Now it was time to eat my meal, which consisted that evening of several tortillas, with nothing on them except a little salt shared by a kindly lady, followed up by two tortillas wrapped around two halves of pumpkin candy. It was a banquet.

I returned early to the jailhouse basement for a clean, but hard, bed. Since I was the first there, I was right next to the warmth of the furnace—and enjoyed a full night's restful sleep.

The following night was my third and final stay as a guest of the San Antonio police. I had spent the preceding day wandering around some more, becoming familiar with the narrow, winding downtown streets. It has been said that the founding fathers laid out the streets to follow the existing Indian and animal paths, which rarely went very far in a straight line. It was easy to believe.

After a free, hot breakfast on South Alamo Street that morning, I picked up a discarded morning newspaper and spotted an advertisement for carhops at Duran's, a Mexican food restaurant on East Josephine Street. I needed no one to tell me what a carhop did. My years as a soda jerker included "hopping" the cars that honked for service at curbside.

With more confidence and hope than I had had for many days, I walked north on Alamo Street, over to the beginning of Broadway at Houston Street, all the way out Broadway to Josephine Street, and then westward a couple of blocks to Duran's place.

There I waited until its early crew arrived, and then I applied to a handsome man for the job. He was the owner's son, Nano Duran, maybe five years my senior. Nano looked me over while I held my breath, hoping my recently laundered clothes would pass the cleanliness test. When Nano learned that I had worked as a soda jerker and was used to dealing with the public, he told me I was hired.

"How much do I get paid?" I asked, now aware this question should always be cleared up in advance. Was I finally beginning to grow up?

"Depends on you," he smiled. "You keep all the tips you make. However, you do have to have a fund to work with. You have to pay for the orders as you take them out to the customer. Then you collect from the customer. You'll need at least a dollar to start this operating fund. Do you have a dollar?"

Crestfallen, I shook my head and started to turn away.

"Don't worry," he cautioned. "See that short, fat man over there? He's going to be your boss on the job. Also, he can be your banker. He'll lend you a dollar each day. You pay him back at night and give him a dime for the use of the dollar. Can you do that?"

"Yes sir," I replied eagerly. "I'm ready to start today."

Start that day I did. Carhop number 21, at Duran's. Other than a small dining room fronting on Josephine Street at that time, it was primarily a drive-in Mexican food restaurant, serving people in cars with a long wooden tray that stretched from one window sill across the driver's lap, ending up on the window on the passenger's side. A similar tray fit the rear seat, but most customers were singles or doubles. Rarely was the back seat occupied. The tray was extendable, so it could fit any width of car. (In later years, Duran's expanded its small dining room and eventually did away with carhops altogether.)

Well, the fat old man, Jose Garcia, financed me each day, all right, and practically every day as long as I worked there. He must have earned a fairly good sum of money in those depression days by bankrolling his "boys." But a manager he was not.

He had no equitable system for assigning customers

89

to his carhops. Instead, we had to stand in a row at the edge and rear of the building by the kitchen, and as a car rounded the corner from Josephine Street, ostensibly to pull into the parking lot in back of the kitchen for food service, the first carhop who yelled his own number got that car for his customer. Mr. Garcia's main function, besides being a money lender, was to act as judge when two or more carhops yelled at the same time.

Even the first evening I became adept at some of the tricks my co-workers used. They would yell when they first spotted a car, whether it was turning in toward us or not. Then, I discovered they were yelling when they merely heard a car approaching, though they would invariably claim they had spotted it about to make its turn in our direction. I got a few customers, and managed to increase my share as days went by.

But tips were small, usually a nickel or dime, and on too many occasions there were none at all. Believe me, we bent over backwards to befriend every customer that we got. I don't remember how much I made that first day, which started about 11 a.m. and lasted until 11 p.m., but it was encouraging. At least I made enough to pay Jose his dime, and possibly thirty or forty cents more.

My immediate problem after work that night was to find a decent place to live. If possible, I preferred to get away from the kind hospitality of the San Antonio Police Department.

When I asked around among the other carhops, one of them, Juan Sanchez, told me his family could rent me a room for a dollar a week. It was located only a few short blocks away, almost opposite the entrance to the Pearl Brewery, dormant since Prohibition except for manufacturing a product called "near beer."

Being in the same business, Juan understood my budget crisis and did not demand payment in advance. So after my first day on the job, I began rooming with this hospitable, Tex-Mex family. For an extra twenty-five cents, the jovial mother would wash my few clothes.

It took a few days for me to learn how carhops survived. They did not spend their hard earned tips on food. The secret was to wait until the evening hours, then target some nice couple, or a pair of lovers who pulled into the place with no real intention of eating.

Half an enchilada, part of a tostada or even a whole, untouched tamale might be left on a number of dishes. As he picked up the trays and carried them towards the kitchen, the carhop would hide the uneaten food dish behind a bush, get fresh utensils from the kitchen, and proceed to finish the meal. Undoubtedly, management was fully aware of this practice, but said and did nothing about it.

I decided I had no choice but to follow suit, as I was never able to earn as much as a dollar a day in tips. This meant that along with most of the others I was eternally borrowing from Mr. Garcia, my banker-boss.

One tall, older fellow from Chicago outdid us all, consistently earning enough to finance his own operating fund. With his height he could see over our heads, and whenever he joined the waiting row of carhops he usually called his number before the rest of us could open our mouths. My "21!" rarely beat his "19!"

But I earned enough so that I was able finally to pay my room rent in advance and to purchase some clothes. On the west side of San Antonio there were a number of second-hand clothing stores. A few coins could purchase serviceable secondhand trousers, a sweater, even "new" shoes. Woolworth's and Kress's, five-and-dime stores, were paradise for poor people for inexpensive underwear, socks, handkerchiefs, shirts and other necessities.

Had the tide turned in my battle with the Great Depression? I felt that it had, as each day I felt more confident that I was going to win. But the fight was not yet over.

"More important than the mistake may be what you do about it afterwards."

— (The Author)

Chapter 10

SHUCKS ... AND ... HOT TAMALES

Life finally fell into a more steady routine, providing a sense of security long missing. I was making friends with the family of my landlord, as well as improving my conversational Spanish, or to be more accurate, my Tex-Mex.

Their family name was Sanchez, about as widespread in the Hispanic world as Smith is in the English. The mother of my working friend Juan — even though a native Texan — never spoke English, forcing me to use my school Spanish, not quite the same as Texas-Mexicans used.

At my Louisiana high school, the Spanish teacher had instructed us in Castilian, the mother tongue of Spain. It had some pronounced differences from Tex-Mex. Nevertheless, I had learned enough of the basic sentence structures and working verbs and nouns common to Spanish speakers worldwide to communicate with more ease as time went by.

By becoming friends and trying to speak in Mother Sanchez's vernacular, I got a very reasonable price for having my few clothes kept clean. And, on occasion, I was invited to breakfast with the family, usually of *huevos rancheros* — eggs covered with chili sauce — for which I formed a lasting fondness. The coffee, though, was weak as dishwater to one raised on the chicory-enhanced variety.

But my landlady, her son and daughter, were most gracious and understanding, not too far removed from the recent poverty from which I had fled. The difference was that everything in the "Alamo city" was incredibly inexpensive. One could live quite well on a few dollars a week if "quite well" means having enough money for the essentials such as food, home and clothing — plus an occasional movie, a picnic in the public park, or attendance at a sports or musical event.

But as it was unusual for someone my age to earn more than a few dollars a week, it proved equally difficult to send money to my family. I may have mailed a dollar or two home, but most of the time I was never far enough ahead to spare a dollar. My goal of giving direct help to my family, and not simply saving them money by not being with them, was as yet unrealized. At least I was not another mouth to be fed by them.

My day at Duran's started at 11 a.m., but since the Sanchez cottage was so close, about three city blocks, I usually showed up as early as 10 or 10:30, unless I spent the morning shopping for clothes and other needed items.

One of the most important of these purchases was stationery on which to write a long-overdue letter to the folks to assure them I was okay, was working, and not to worry about me — and finally to supply them with my correct return address. Their reply showed their relief. In fact, I began writing descriptions of the wonders of the big city I now called home, dwelling at length on the mixture of two main cultures: Anglo and Mexican or Spanish. I had not as yet fully discerned the extent of the early German and Czech settlers' influence.

My primary concern now was to stabilize my situation. I was not interested in job opportunities elsewhere, at least at the moment. Most of my fellow carhops were a little older than I. One in particular was the tall youth from Chicago who consistently edged us out on the carhop calling line. He was very outgoing, even a braggart, about his life in the windy city. For some reason he never revealed why he had deserted such a heaven to come to San Antonio, and, of course, we didn't ask.

I gradually became better acquainted with another carhop, a native San Antonian named Bobby Whittridge, who was about my age. Usually we chatted near the end of our twelve-hour shifts, with most of the day's income tucked away in our pockets. Bobby had finished high school, and in an incautious moment I confessed that I had not, that I had left home to find work before my final half-year. For some reason this intrigued Bobby, who became more inquisitive as the days passed.

We were allowed one day off each week, usually a Monday or Tuesday, the least busy days. When our off-days coincided after a couple of weeks, Bobby invited me to his home for dinner. I accepted, and here again I encountered the friendliness that I have always associated with San Antonio.

Bobby's widowed mother was warmly sympathetic to my circumstances and asked prying questions that I did not resent. An older sister of Bobby's was the household's principal breadwinner, with Bobby's meager income making a difference. Their home, in a modest neighborhood, was considerably more affluent than the one I was rooming in, so obviously they had once seen better times.

The dinner laid out for me seemed a sumptuous banquet, especially since my customary big meal of the day consisted of untouched food from the trays of my customers. A "gringo" can become a little tired of a straight diet of frijoles, tortillas, enchiladas, tacos, enchimales, tamales, tostadas, and chili. I had yet to discover the one Mexican food that became my all-time favorite: *mole poblano* or chicken mole (chicken breast covered with a delicious sauce that contains, among its other ingredients, enough raw chocolate to impart a distinctive, unique flavor).

It was shortly after this visit to Bobby's home that he confided he had been looking into the possibility of a better-paying job and thought he had a chance for one at a bookbindery. I didn't know what a bookbindery was exactly, so I paid little heed at the time. I had cause to recall this conversation later.

On the carhop line, I was becoming more accomplished at acquiring customers but never succeeded in clearing as much as a dollar a day, and thus rarely, if ever, equalled the five dollars weekly salary earned at my Pineville drugstore job. But I did continue to enrich our carhop manager with his daily ten cent fee for the use of his dollar. The big days usually were on Friday nights, Saturdays and Sundays. The best customers were amorous couples, who failed to finish even half their orders before they would depart for some lovers' lane in nearby Brackenridge Park and usually were a little more generous with their tips.

Then I managed to accumulate some money ahead and began to believe that it would soon be possible to get away from the daily dime tribute to Jose Garcia. But alas, about that time bad luck struck. I had the misfortune to get for one of my customers a man who placed a big order — two complete dinners. He "got" me instead.

He failed to honk his horn to signal that he was through, so I could retrieve the tray and pick up his payment for the meals. He simply started his vehicle and without turning on his lights eased out onto Josephine Street and took off with the tray and all the food and dishes rattling around on it. Evidently, finding himself broke and unable to pay, he had sneaked off, thus cheating me not only out of the price of his meals, but also adding a charge for the missing dishes and tray.

By this time I had made a fairly good impression on Nano Duran, who usually ran the kitchen and the cash register on weekends. He charged me a token sum for the dishes, and though he could have added the missing tray to the tab, he didn't. With even a small loss like this, I was in debt for many days and at the continued mercy of my daily financier. From then on I kept a sharper eye on my customers. At the sound of any motor, I was quick to determine if it was my customer taking off. Luckily the incident was not repeated.

The next mishap occurred one busy evening as I was bringing in a customer's tray with empty dishes. I accidentally bumped into another carhop on his way out with a loaded tray. I recovered my balance but not in time to prevent a small dish from falling onto a concrete ledge surrounding shrubbery near the door. It shattered into pieces as it struck the concrete. I continued on in and turned the tray over to Nano Duran, who said nothing as he accepted it.

I turned around, went outside, picked up the broken

96

pieces, brought them back in and handed them to Nano, saying, "I just broke this; I'll pay for it."

Nano smiled. "I saw what happened. Forget it, but be careful going in and out the door."

A few days after the broken dish episode, as I was waiting for the 11 a.m. opening, Nano came to the door and motioned me inside.

"How would you like an extra job?" he asked. "No money, but it will get you a big breakfast each day."

I eagerly nodded yes.

"Okay, you've got it," he said. "You're honest, and that's why I'm doing this. Get here by 9:30 tomorrow morning, and I'll show you what I want you to do."

Promptly at 9:30 the next morning I knocked on the back door of Duran's and was escorted by Nano to the upstairs storage room where an ancient Texas-Mexican introduced me to one of the essential steps in the manufacture of the homemade tamales for which Duran's was famous.

The step was simple but tedious. Take an ear of corn from a bin, remove the shucks, separate and throw away the topmost shuck, examine the one under it for "livestock" — worms, etc. — of any kind, as well as dirt. If clean, put this one in the acceptable pile. If not clean, and a little brushing doesn't work, discard that one and go down another layer to another shuck and repeat. Do this long enough to accumulate a pile of acceptable shucks a foot or so high. Then take the pile in a basket downstairs to the tamale cook, who takes over and expertly wraps each shuck around a tamale awaiting this sheath before it can be placed in the pot and steamed into a delicious hot tamale.

In those days, a genuine corn shuck served as the jacket for each tamale. And I had become an authentic "hot tamale corn shuck cleaner."

My reward each morning was a choice of *huevos rancheros* or anything else on the menu. Breakfast became my big meal of the day. It cut down most of my need to rob customers' trays of untouched food, which I was happy to forego.

Being thus allowed into the inner sanctum of the kitchen, I particularly noticed one piece of equipment that really stood out. It was a mechanical dishwasher, probably one of the earliest made for restaurants. It was slow and

97

cumbersome and took up an inordinate amount of space, but it worked.

As I watched it cleanse every bit of food particles from each plate with strong jets of steaming hot water, memories of my three days as a dishwasher in that oil boomtown in East Texas came to mind. This mechanical dishwasher was what my Gladewater boss needed, rather than a replacement for me.

As I settled into a comfortable daily routine I felt more strongly that the tide of battle had definitely turned in my favor, that perhaps this could be considered another round and that I was winning on points. At least I was surviving. I began to smile, laugh and joke with my co-workers. At the same time, I realized my battle with the Great Depression was far from over, though I did not have apprehensions about the final outcome. I was determined to win. Was I overly optimistic?

Car hopping at Duran's in San Antonio, Texas, was far different from soda jerking at the Owl Drugstore in Pineville, Louisiana, pictured here.

"Laughter does not fill an empty stomach ... "
-- (Anonymous)

Chapter 11

HOW TO HANDLE DIRTY BOOKS

I liked my new extra duties as a shuck cleaner. No one hassled me, urging me to speed it up. I took my time and did the job right. And Nano Duran was pleased with the quality of my work. He praised me for taking time "to clean 'em right." Both the praise and the "free" breakfast were greatly appreciated. A little pat on the back and food in the belly goes far toward making a happier, satisfied employee.

It was now around mid-November, shortly after a new president, that Yankee farmer named Roosevelt, had been elected. The mood of almost everybody that I came in contact with had brightened. President "Ruzzvelt," as most folks hereabouts pronounced the name, had promised to lead us out of our dismal depression. Hope was in the air.

Even my rotund landlady became more cheerful. She was confident that after the new president took office, steps would be taken to bring back legal beer. This would awaken the long dormant Pearl Brewery across the street from her house. This meant the brewery would soon be hiring her neighbors and friends, and eventually even her son when he reached the minimum age allowed to work around alcoholic beverages. She began to sing her Mexican folk songs more often and with more lilt and energy.

In the meantime, autumn winds were changing the climate of sunny San Antonio. In anticipation, I slowly built up a small wardrobe of heavier clothes, but I knew I'd need more to withstand the coming chill of winter — if winters here were anything like I was used to. And that, in turn, meant it would be helpful if there were more money available to make these purchases. Hence, when Bobby Whittridge told me he had landed an indoors job at a business called the Universal Bookbindery, my ears perked up. I wanted to know more about it.

He painted a glowing picture: there was no outside work in all kinds of weather such as we had at Duran's and one sat in comfort under a roof while performing his task. Also, it was a piecework operation. Payment was based on the number of renovated books one was able to turn out. A good worker could earn more than a dollar a day, he assured me.

This prospect entranced me. I liked handling books, and I had never earned more than a dollar a day in my life. Was this the opportunity I was waiting for?

I wanted to find out.

On my next day off I made my way to the large building that housed the bookbindery. As I listened to the personnel manager's spiel, I boldly decided to apply for the job on the spot.

It was pleasant to be told immediately that my application was accepted. Of course, I informed my new employer that I would have to give notice to my present one.

Nano Duran was encouraging. "Work here as long as you like, or quit tomorrow, if it will help you. You don't need to give us more notice than this."

I showed up at the bookbindery the next day, ready to get started on my first million. Books, that is, not dollars. Directed to the second floor, I introduced myself to an elderly lady supervisor whose desk faced an entire floor filled with industrious-looking workers, sitting at their desks busily thumbing through stacks of books piled high in front of them.

The supervisor explained the set-up. The bindery

had a contract with various public school systems to take students' scribbled-on, torn and dilapidated schoolbooks — in other words, dirty books — and then refurbish, renovate or do whatever was necessary to them, so they could be put back into use for another batch of students.

I had recently come from Louisiana, where free schoolbooks were fairly new. Until Huey P. Long made it a political issue, parents were required to purchase all schoolbooks used by their children. Apparently Texas had been way ahead of Louisiana in providing free books to its public school students.

As I started in on this cleanup job, the sheer number of dirty, mutilated books surprised me. Were we perhaps a little more careful in Louisiana with these important educational tools than the kids in San Antonio and surrounding counties?

The bookbindery's procedure to fulfill its contracts seemed simple enough. Each worker received a desk full of old schoolbooks, damaged and marked up by the users. The refurbisher's task was to go through each dirty book looking for pencil marks, handwriting, etc., and then erase them.

We were to clean them up as much as possible and also look for damaged and missing pages, which we were then to tape, if possible, or replace. When we found missing or pages too badly torn, we replaced them with duplicate pages from a book that was kept for that purpose (the boneyard, I called it). The bindery was paid by the school system customer on the basis of each book renovated for further use.

I never found out what the bindery received for each resurrection, but this process must have saved taxpayers a considerable sum. The worker was paid for each book saved, but the amount varied depending on the type of book. Small books brought in a few pennies. Larger, thicker ones paid a few pennies more. The key to a larger income was the speed with which a worker could make his product presentable enough to pass the supervisor's eagle eyes.

I lunched with Bobby Whittridge on that first day on the new job. He led me down the street past the Alamo and the Menger Hotel, on past a famous department store then known as Joske's, to Commerce Street. East on Commerce in back of Joske's was a row of small businesses, one of which was a hole-in-the-wall restaurant with the fascinating Great Depression name of "A Fast Nickel Beats a Slow Dime."

Everything there cost only a nickel. Perhaps the bowl they served my nickel chili in was not as large as a regular bowl, or my glass of milk a standard size, but the small slice of pecan pie for desert made the meal a perfectly satisfying one — a fifteen-cent lunch that turned out to be my biggest meal of the day for many days thereafter.

Also, a chain of drugstores known as Sommers dotted the city and were conveniently located. They provided a satisfying breakfast at fantastically low prices for many years — an egg with bacon, toast with jelly and a cup of coffee for only nineteen cents in 1932, gradually going up a penny or so at a time in the waning years of the Depression.

My urgent task was to earn enough for the Sommers breakfast and the "Fast Nickel" lunch, plus enough to cover the dollar-per-week rent and the twenty-five-cent clothes laundering. If I did this I could survive, and by slowly building up my small wardrobe, I could improve my lot in life. But would I ever get enough ahead to send some to the folks back home?

My progress at the bindery went at a snail's pace. I seemed never able to avoid looking at every page in the book I was working on. I felt a compulsion to erase every pencil mark, no matter how small. Once a dishwasher, always a dishwasher! Leave no scraps on the plate, nor blemish in the book!

I realized that if I were to earn as much as a dollar a day, I would have to bring back to life at least thirty or forty or more schoolbooks a day. I was finding this hard to accomplish, and not simply because of my tidiness. The books themselves, as well as their contents, were interesting, and more than once I found myself reading a fascinating page or paragraph from a textbook on the history of Texas, or some other interesting part of the world.

I plugged away at the bookbindery through the remainder of November, trying to increase my renovating speed. Even though they had been at the task much longer, my co-workers continued to surprise me with how fast they processed a book. They recognized the difficulty I was having, and from time to time would kiddingly tell me that I was too particular, that I should skip the minor marks that dirtied a book.

Finally, I decided to see if I could lower my personal standards to increase my output. I experimented with one book, intentionally leafing quickly through it, concentrating mainly on torn and missing pages. When I turned it in to the supervisor for inspection, it was rejected, returned to me to redo without comment.

I couldn't bring myself to try short cuts again, though some of those around me who were honestly concerned with my lack of progress, continued to urge me to do so. They whispered that on average the supervisor couldn't check too closely each and every book.

But it began to dawn on me that I couldn't make it. I was probably the slowest worker there. It was time to face reality.

Bobby invited me to his home for Thanksgiving, and I took this occasion to tell him my doubts about surviving at the bindery, much less getting ahead in life and moving toward something better. Sympathetic as he was, he was unable to suggest any alternatives, at least at the moment.

So after only a couple of weeks on the job, to do some private thinking on my situation I took a Sunday hike along the then unpaved, downtown banks of the San Antonio River. This stroll unexpectedly led to my learning a major lesson: check all the facts before making a decision that will change one's direction in life.

On this casual walk I chanced to meet a youth about my age or a year older, whom I instantly recognized as being from Pineville. He was hard to forget, with his lean, tall figure, dark complexion and hair. He could pass as a Mexican-American, though I knew that he was not. He had been a year ahead of me in Bolton High, and we were only nodding acquaintances there.

He recognized me, too, and we shook hands as if we were the best of friends. After we briefed each other about how we had landed in San Antonio, he persuaded me to go into business with him. The state of my mind at that critical moment was especially receptive to his proposition.

Unfortunately, his project was just the type of enterprise that appealed to me: secondhand books and magazines. He was bent on starting a used book and magazine store, off the main streets in San Antonio. He admitted he

103

had very little capital, but he finally convinced me that all we had to do in the beginning was knock on enough doors and ask people to donate their unwanted books and used magazines to our cause.

He was staying with a relative in San Antonio who would provide enough money for the rent, to start us off, or so he informed me. I should have checked out this "fact" in advance, but I didn't, to my later regret.

The following day I gave a week's notice at the bindery. Then, my friend (whom I'll call Henry) and I began knocking on doors in the more affluent section of the city. Indeed, we did have success in acquiring used periodicals and a few books when we took the time to explain to the housewife what our ambitious plans were. San Antonians were friendly and encouraging toward teenagers going into business for themselves!

But the key person to be sold on the merits of our venture was Henry's relative, and she wasn't convinced. After three days of our knocking on doors, Henry met me with a long face and mournfully confessed that our undertaking was on the rocks. Without the help he had been expecting, there was nothing further to be done. Henry shook my hand and said good-by. I never saw nor heard from him again.

I contacted my friend Bobby Whittridge before the day was out, and related the sad tale. He was sympathetic, even said he was sure I could go back to the bookbindery. But a blind, juvenile streak in me prevented my even thinking of doing so.

I was sure I could also go back to Duran's, if they were not overflowing with carhops, and if I really wanted to. But I was not yet desperate enough to retreat; to my young mind, retreat meant defeat in my battle versus the Great Depression.

My rent was paid up for a few more days, but complications had set in with Juan and his little family. He had left Duran's before me, for another job that had not panned out either. He was in the same stew as I.

In fact, he was even worse off, since all their money had been used up, even my rent money, and there was practically no food at all in his household.

I had some coins left, and after I discovered Juan's

problems, I bought several bunches of carrots that were on sale very cheaply at a local grocery and presented them to Juan's mother. I had always liked carrots and had been told their carotene was excellent for eyesight and general health.

As a result of my little gift, I was invited to help consume these carrots, and for all of three days while I was reading want ads along with Juan, we lived off those carrots. It has been said that if one must eat something exclusively for a long enough period of time, one begins to hate it. Well, we ate them raw, stewed, fried, baked, you name it, and yet I have never lost my desire for this tasty nutritious vegetable.

Meanwhile, I had noticed from the ads that there was a constant demand for newsboys — "hawkers" as they were sometimes called. I had read most of Horatio Alger's books about lads who started out as newsboys and then became great American success stories. Had the tide turned against me in this round with the Great Depression? Perhaps, but having made a promise that I would consider every possibility rather than throw in the towel, I chose to explore this avenue. To ignore it might force a resumption of hobo existence, in which event this round would definitely go against me.

In the first week of December in response to its ads, I called on the *San Antonio Light* at its headquarters on Broadway, only a couple of blocks from the bookbindery. I was immediately referred by the front desk to Ramon, the circulation supervisor in charge of a section in the heart of downtown supervising a number of newsboys making street sales. After a few minutes' talk with Ramon, I had become the newest member of his crew.

Good-by, dirty books! Move over, Horatio Alger, Jr. Though I didn't know it at the time, this was the step that would lead me out of the doldrums of indecision and the misery of poverty — and to final victory over the Great Depression.

105

"The ... crash of 1929 ... still affects all our lives today."
— **Gordon Thomas & Max Morgan-Witts**

Chapter 12

"DON'T YELL SO LOUD. I CAN'T WORK!"

The following day I was standing at my first "news station," on the northwest corner of Broadway and Houston Streets, right in front of a Sommers drugstore. Ramon broke me in to the art and science of selling newspapers at this location by putting me under the tutelage of an experienced vendor.

After two days he moved me a half block west so that I was hawking papers by myself on the north side of Houston Street across from an office building known as the Maverick building.

The method of paying news hawkers on the front line, as I was, was on a piecework basis. The daily paper sold for two cents, so I earned one cent for every one I sold. To earn a dollar a day, I only had to sell 100 papers.

A sales gimmick newspapers used was to publish several editions daily. The news might not be different from one edition to the next, but headlines were recycled differently to make it appear so.

These multiple editions gave the newsboys a shot at

selling more than one paper a day to the same customer — as well as adding to the paper's total circulation, which was as important then as it is now in attracting advertisers.

If sales were slow, I was advised to get sensational with the hawking! I was instructed that it was not against the law to yell: "Get your latest news. Baby born with a mustache!" or some equally implausible utterance. We rarely had time to glance inside the product we hawked, but if we caught any hint of a sensational news story on the inside or back pages, a murder or a sex scandal, for example, we yelled it out loudly.

I was not unduly surprised one day when a little grey-haired lady collared me, pulled me to one side out of the way of the passing throng, and said sternly, "Young man, can't you find something nice to yell about?" She then let me go, turned and walked away, obviously disgusted with all newsboys.

For the remainder of that day, I tried very hard to locate anything in the paper that was "nice" to shout about, but I couldn't find a thing!

And, alas, I was never able to sell a hundred papers on a weekday. My earnings varied, but I usually made fifty to seventy-five cents, which was enough to get by on at the cheap places I knew about.

The bonanza came on Saturdays. The *Light* had an advanced printing of its Sunday edition, so that some time after noon on Saturdays I was able to leave my spot on Houston Street and go to the *Light* headquarters to pick up an armful of the Sunday papers. I would then stride through some residential section yelling "Get your Sunday *Light* today!"

Many people, even today in San Antonio, still read their Sunday *Light* on Saturdays. I certainly did, I always kept one copy for myself, which I read from cover to cover in bed on Saturday night before falling asleep.

The bonanza lay in the price of that Saturday "Sunday" edition: several times the price of the daily. If memory serves me right, it may have been five or even ten cents a copy. I still made half of the selling price on each one I sold, so I only had to sell a relatively smaller number to earn a dollar. I came close a couple of times, but never quite made it. Still, these extra Saturday afternoon and evening sales of the Sunday edition gave a healthy boost to my income.

Had it been possible to hawk the papers on Sunday, I might have made my goal, but Sundays were truly a day of rest. No hawking! Only regular routemen and newsstands sold then.

While working my spot on Houston Street one day, I noticed a portly man eyeing me. Finally, he came over and said he was impressed with my news-hawking ability, that he was on the editorial staff at *Light* headquarters and was interested in hiring on a promising assistant. "Come and see me when you knock off at dusk, and let's talk," he said. He told me his name and where to meet him, then walked away quickly.

This editorial staffer failed to spot Ramon, who was watching from the doorway of the drugstore. After the man went up Broadway far enough to be out of sight, Ramon strolled over and asked me what the man had said. I told him.

"He's a 'queer.' He's after you, so don't go," Ramon cautioned. The man was well-known to most of the experienced newsboys, Ramon said, and then he revealed some details of what could happen if I were to accept the invitation.

This was a strange and unfamiliar world I was learning about. Needless to say, I did not accept the invitation; in fact I steered as clear as possible from *Light* headquarters from then on.

It seemed like forever, but at the end of my second week Ramon said he'd like to put me in a new place that had never been effectively worked before. It would be directly in front of the entrance to the Maverick building facing Nueva Street.

It was only a small office building no more than six or seven stories high. Ramon assured me that I was coming along fine, and he thought I could in time increase my sales at the new spot (and incidentally increase his overall income, as he was paid on the basis of the total sales of his crew).

Thus, at the beginning of my third full week, my personal bailiwick became the entrance to the Maverick building and its immediate area.

The first day I didn't do as well as at my former stand on Houston Street. But it was a challenge, so I went back the second day and yelled my head off, trying to up my score.

Sales improved as I kept at it energetically.

One day in the midst of a headline-yelling spree, I felt a hand on my shoulder, turned around and saw a bespectacled, red-faced, stocky man in a business suit.

In a firm voice he said, "Christ, son, don't yell so loud. I can't get any work done because of your yelling."

I silently nodded assent. Without a further word, the gentleman turned back into the Maverick building. After he had vanished, I wondered aloud: "Which office is he in?"

A man standing nearby spoke up, "It's on the top floor. That was Maury Maverick, young man."

I still wondered, but now to myself: "*Who* is Maury Maverick?"

(It would take a couple of years or so for me to get the full answer to that question. Eventually I would meet Maury Maverick, who later became the Congressman from San Antonio, in more pleasant surroundings and circumstances. This would occur through a mutual friend, ex-state Senator Harry Hertzberg — the same Hertzberg for whom that Circus Museum only three blocks south of the Maverick building would be named, located in the City Library that I had entered on my very first day in San Antonio.)

About a week before Christmas a letter came from my mother. She had some surprising news: I had a relative in San Antonio, Mr. Conley B. Stroud, her cousin!

Mother was a Claunch and the Claunch family had lived in Northeast Louisiana since the 1850s. There were many daughters, and they had intermarried with other pioneer families of Louisiana. One of the Claunches had married into the Stroud line and C. B. was one of the children.

Mother had busily written to her relatives from the day she had received my first letter from San Antonio. She had learned that cousin Conley lived somewhere on Laclede Street and was a cook for a large drugstore chain.

The main kitchen for all the Sommers drugstores was located in the short block on Nueva Street between my newspaper territory and the San Antonio River. The luncheon meals were prepared at this location and delivered daily to each store in the chain. There was a good chance that cousin Conley worked in that kitchen, only a stone's throw from where I paced my daily station. I could hardly wait until the next day to get back to my newspaper beat; in fact,

110

I arrived early, before the early edition had been dumped off for me.

When I entered Sommer's modern, massive kitchen, I was greeted with a sea of white. Everywhere people wearing white uniforms and aprons were scurrying around performing various tasks, so a few moments passed before someone noticed me near the door, came over and asked what I wanted.

"To see Mr. Stroud," I replied. In a moment I was conversing with the head cook of all this orderly confusion, cousin Conley B. Stroud, outfitted in a white uniform like the rest of his crew.

He was not surprised to see me. Word had gotten to him from our mutual relatives that his cousin Blanch Claunch Edwards had been searching for her runaway son who was now reported to be in the Alamo city. He gave me a welcoming handshake, said he couldn't talk long, as this was his busiest time of day, and concluded by inviting me to spend Christmas Day with his family.

I accepted with alacrity. San Antonio, the friendly city, now seemed friendlier and warmer all the time. Any remaining thoughts I had about a faraway place called Brazil had long since vanished from my plans.

I went about my paper-selling with renewed zest that day, though moderating the volume of my voice when in front of the Maverick building so as not to prevent that gentleman on the top floor from working. I even developed a new technique. In front of the Maverick building was Nueva, a two-way north-south street. At its intersection with Houston was a traffic signal, where vehicles sometimes backed up all the way to College Street, the next street south, when the light was red for northbound traffic.

I began to hawk my papers while running alongside the backed-up line of cars. When I reached the end of the line, I swung back to my sidewalk territory and walked rapidly along it to Houston Street, selling to pedestrians as I went. By the time I reached Houston Street, the light was red again for traffic on Nueva, so I repeated the run alongside the cars, completing the circuit.

It kept me busy, but it increased my sales by ten to twenty percent a day. I went for those extra pennies with a vengeance. When Christmas Day rolled around, I could

111

afford to take the southbound streetcar to a suburb known as Harlandale. I got off at Laclede Street, walked quickly and confidently to the Stroud home, and found a warmth and friendship that I cherished for many years. A wonderful home-cooked meal, turkey with all the trimmings, did much to add to this warmth.

Among the Strouds' other guests were long-time friends, the Heards, a family with a vivacious young daughter, Inez. Her energy, friendliness and beauty captivated me so much that for the first time in my life I dared to ask a girl for a date.

The Strouds even had a Christmas package for me. Cousin Conley may have been very busy the day I met him, but he was a careful observer for he presented me with a couple of pairs of new socks. Had my fortunes not improved within a very short time after this, I am confident that Cousin Conley would have found some way to rescue me from the increasing chill on the streets of San Antonio. I felt he was that kind of man, but as long as I was making it on my own I had no wish to ask for help.

As to Cousin Conley's thoughtful Christmas gift, weeks earlier, when I had first acquired some extra money, I had added some inexpensive socks to my wardrobe. But that had been a while ago when I was at Duran's, and cheap socks wear out quickly. Also, I had learned along the way that when holes appeared in the heels of my socks, I could make do awhile longer by inverting the socks, putting them on with the heel on my instep — that is, when I wore socks at all. Most people never seemed to notice, at least they made no comment on my holey socks, as the heel was barely visible unless I stooped over or sat down and my foot and shoe came into clear view. Obviously Cousin Conley had noticed and realized the needs of a lone teenage boy in the Great Depression.

(When the new socks began to wear out, I treated them no differently than the others. Years later, close friends convinced me that with the Great Depression over I need no longer engage in this peculiar practice.)

112

"If you give luck a chance, sometimes it rewards you."
— Tony Hillerman

Chapter 13

"WOULD YOU LIKE TO BE A LAWYER?"

Following the heartwarming Christmas with the Strouds, I really started to think of myself as a San Antonian. My father was a native Texan; so if he was a "longhorn," couldn't I be at least a half-Texan, a "shorthorn"?

I wrote the folks back home more often now, telling them all about our San Antonio cousins, of Christmas Day with them, and about the general atmosphere of friendliness that existed in this "little Spanish town" that had captivated me so completely.

Often my thoughts were about the folks back home, especially Dad. I really could not determine how he was doing from the noncommittal letters that reached me. But from the general tone of what Mother wrote, it didn't seem they were any better off. I could only imagine what kind of a Christmas they had in Louisiana in 1932.

By this time, my younger sister Oletta had been compelled to drop out of school and go to work in a five-and-dime store in Alexandria. This news made me feel less guilty that I left home with half a year to go to complete high school. It verified to me that my decision to leave was correct; had I remained, I too would have been forced out of school.

Before my sister dropped out, she wrote that her Spanish teacher at Bolton High (which she had reentered when the family moved back to Pineville), who had also been my teacher, promised her an "A" if I would write a letter about my experiences speaking Spanish in San Antonio. I never complied with Oletta's request, although I had the best intentions of doing so. Even if I had, her "A" grade still would not have kept her in school, so perhaps she has forgiven me. Besides, I later learned that she earned an A on her own ability anyhow.

The week following Christmas up through New Year's was traditionally slow for all kinds of businesses. But to survive, I had to continue what I was doing, and I did it the best I knew how, except, of course, that I still lowered my voice somewhat so as not to disturb the gentleman on the top floor of the Maverick building.

Not only did I occasionally see cousin Conley, but I began to recognize and speak with a few of the other regulars in the area. Just beyond the Sommers kitchen, there was a very small open parking lot. It was operated by a Mr. Davies, who managed to eke out a small living for himself and his family from this 12-car parking spot.

Mr. Davies was from the New York/New Jersey area, down on his luck because of the effects of the Great Depression. He had been a corporate officer for the Lykes steamship line and it must have been his strong Welsh heritage that saved him from leaping from a tall building when Wall Street crashed. Like me, he didn't believe in throwing in the towel. He had brought his family to inexpensive San Antonio and started all over again.

A regular customer of mine was a man who lived in the small, six-story Hotel Palms, cater-cornered from the Maverick building, fronting on College Street with back stairs leading down to the banks of the San Antonio River. (Eventually this structure was converted into an apartment building, with a famous seafood restaurant on its lower levels.)

After unobtrusively observing my pacing up and down my sales territory, this gentleman finally introduced himself as Walter D. Queed, a civil service worker at Kelly Air Force Base and also a part-time lawyer. He usually bought one of the last papers of the day from me, on his way home from his Air Force job.

At first I didn't understand how a person could earn enough money to maintain a home in a hotel. I was soon to learn. One evening right after New Year's he invited me to go to dinner with him. I had to think this over very carefully, after my earlier encounter with a stranger, so I told him I was tied up that evening.

This gave me the opportunity next morning to inquire about him from my sales supervisor Ramon. Ramon had sold papers and supervised a crew of newshawks in this area for a number of years, so when he gave Mr. Queed a clean bill of health, I felt relieved.

To check all the facts, however, I walked down to the next block and talked with Mr. Davies, whom I had noticed on several occasions chatting with Mr. Queed.

"He's a Mason, Duval," Mr. Davies said. "That's an organization that encourages its members to be devoted to charitable work. I think you ought to accept his invitation if he offers it again. You have nothing to lose. He may have some job in mind for you that would get you off the street and out of this weather."

This was a compelling reason to accept Mr. Queed's invitation. Even though winter in San Antonio was not nearly as cold as I suspected it must be in Dallas about this time, the wet, rainy days coupled with the moderately cold temperature went through my thin clothes like a knife at times.

So the next time Mr. Queed walked by and bought his paper, I blurted out that I had nothing on for that evening. He laughed good-heartedly and said he'd be back in a few minutes and we'd go eat.

We wound up on the south end of Alamo Plaza, at a restaurant called "French's Black Cat." It was anything but a quiet place to eat and talk at the same time, but Mr. Queed had pumped me for personal information as we walked the few blocks from the Maverick building.

Since Mr. Queed had received high marks from Mr. Davies, I answered his questions truthfully, though I didn't volunteer anything at first.

"Can you type?" he finally asked.

"Yes sir!" I replied. Now I was excited enough to pour out the whole story of how I'd taught myself the

115

preceding spring, on an old machine my favorite school teacher at Bolton had encouraged me to acquire.

"Okay," he said enthusiastically, "after dinner I want you to come visit me, and let's talk about a different job for you."

I enjoyed that dinner immensely. The Black Cat was one of those places that gains a nationwide reputation not for the quality of its food necessarily, but for the quantity. Mr. Queed rightly figured a growing teenager needed lots of food. For thirty-five cents, I ate one of the largest meals of my life, including milk and an ample slice of San Antonio's famous pecan ("puh-khan") pie.

Somewhat apprehensively, I accompanied Mr. Queed back to his hotel. As we entered the lobby, I spied a man and a woman dressed in some kind of a uniform, both standing behind the reception desk. Mr. Queed introduced me to Captain and Mrs. Parker, stating, "This is the young man you may have seen in front of the Maverick Building, the one I was telling you about."

As each of them shook my hand, I saw the insignia of the Salvation Army on their uniforms. They sounded genuinely pleased to meet me. By now such a friendly reception in San Antonio seemed normal. We went upstairs via the lone elevator, which Mr. Queed operated himself, to the sixth floor and on around the corridor to the very south end of the building. His corner room was the last one, and it overlooked the bend of the river below.

It was a single room, in which Mr. Queed had managed to combine bedroom and office. Against one wall was a desk with a typewriter, and there were a few law books on shelves above it. His law license was prominently displayed on the wall. There were a number of other plaques and framed objects which indicated long association with the Masons.

He invited me to sit at the desk and tackle his typewriter. After a few minutes, he stopped me, looked over my shoulder and said, "That looks pretty good to me. You're faster than I am. I type by the finger method. I only wonder if you can properly type a legal document."

He then handed me a legal form to copy, with the heading of "Plaintiff's Original Petition" visible under the style of a case and the designation of a District Court.

116

I tried to duplicate it exactly, taking more care this time. It was a petition in a divorce case. What I did seemed to satisfy him. We then had a frank discussion about whether I could handle his typing chores on the law cases he handled as a part-time lawyer, and what salary I would need.

It developed that for the most part he handled divorce cases, having a pipeline to clients through his membership in Masonic orders as well as contacts at the Air Force base. None of his cases apparently were too involved, so that he was able to handle them on one of his days off from his Federal Government job.

His proposition: If I would handle all of his typing needs and answer his phone while he was at work, he was prepared to pay me the princely sum of three dollars a week, plus a room of my own at the hotel, which he would rent for me from the Salvation Army for two dollars a week. "Could you live on that?" he asked. As I sat, calculating mentally, he hesitated a moment, then added: "In addition, of course, I could throw in a few meals a week for you."

That added inducement was the clincher.

My two-dollar room looked like it had never been used before. It was adjacent to the one elevator, and therefore noisy, which wasn't often during sleeping hours. The room had only one tiny window which did not look directly on the river scene below, as Mr. Queed's did. But I took it. To me, it was beautiful. I was only a few doors from my job. I was inside during the day. And I was on a regular salary, small as it may have seemed years later.

It turned out that the hotel was owned and operated as a money-making endeavor by the Salvation Army, which did not advertise its ownership in an effort to maintain a quality "commercial" hotel rather than let it become a "flop" house for the poor.

The next morning before I was to report for my first bundle of newspapers, I packed up my few belongings in a bag, said good-by and "Muchas gracias" to my Tex-Mex friends in front of the Pearl Brewery, and moved into Hotel Palms. Then I worked out my last day for Ramon, and told him farewell and thanks.

Mr. Queed had not explained to me why my salary was so low, though by all appearances he was earning a better than average income, regularly. But San Antonio

117

being one of the most inexpensive places to live, a dollar went a long way and I felt sure I could manage. In bidding farewell to my Tex-Mex landlady, I was losing the benefit of her laundry service, but I had priced the regular commercial laundries and was confident I could handle them. Besides, in those days, I was not the only person in the city who wore a shirt for more than one or two days, or underwear either. (In later times, it became much easier for a single person to do essential laundering in a wash basin, but neither the fabrics nor the soaps made the job quite that easy in those olden days.)

One evening as I sat typing a petition for Mr. Queed while he read in his easy chair, I got the answer to my unspoken question about my salary. We had a visitor, a man possibly ten years older than I. Mr. Queed introduced him as Reynolds Andricks (famous years later as the innovator and moving force behind San Antonio's magnificently lighted night parade during fiesta week).

Mr. Queed and Reynolds Andricks talked about Reynolds' wife and young baby and Reynolds' current business prospects. They sounded and talked like family.

After Reynolds left, Mr. Queed filled me in. When Mr. Queed arrived in the Alamo city during World War I, he boarded with the Andricks family. When the father died, Mr. Queed stayed on, and he grew fond of the energetic young Reynolds to the point that he assisted him financially all the way through college.

When Reynolds' mother passed away, Mr. Queed, in effect, was the only family Reynolds had. After he graduated as a civil engineer, during the early Depression years, the only work he could get that was close to his training was an occasional surveying job. While he struggled to get on his feet, especially after he married, Reynolds leaned heavily on Mr. Queed for financial assistance.

So that was the reason Mr. Queed hadn't offered me a better starting salary, though I learned later that there were professional legal secretaries working six days a week in San Antonio for a salary as low as three dollars.

I fell into a routine of entering Mr. Queed's room after he left for his Air Force job and sitting at his desk to practice typing unless he had left a handwritten petition or other pleading for me to copy. His legal practice was very limited,

118

so I had lots of time to read.

I selected a thick book with the title of *Blackstone's Commentaries* as my first read. It seemed even thicker than *Darwin's Origin of the Species* which I had managed to wade through three summers before. It contained extremely technical material about the development of the common law of England, said to be the foundation of the law in practically all of our states with the exception of Louisiana, and to a lesser extent Texas; for that reason, it was compulsory study in law schools. Heavy reading it was, but I found it interesting.

Mr. Queed had some lighter reading material about the law that I enjoyed between heavy bouts with *Blackstone* — especially a series of stories by Arthur Train, about a law firm named *Tutt & Mr. Tutt*, located in a large northern city. These stories about the practice of law in the large metropolis captivated me and probably were as instrumental as my reading of *Blackstone* in directing my future path.

After a few weeks on the job, I had started to get bored because there was so little work, until the day Mr. Queed came in a little early and found me with *Blackstone* in my hands. He was intrigued.

"How do you like it?" he asked.

"It's tough reading, but it's interesting."

"How would you like to be a lawyer?" he asked.

I had never thought of the possibility. Not having finished high school, as by now he was well aware, I knew that I did not have the basic qualifications to enter college, though all my high school courses had been college prep ones.

But on the other hand, being a typist for the rest of my life didn't appeal to me.

"I don't know how I could become one," I replied.

"No problem," he said cheerfully.

Then he poured out information about how I could become a lawyer in three years — provided I finished high school first. It dawned on me that this was probably my best chance, even my last one, to obtain a college degree, the first in my family to do so. Even though midterm classes had already started, I told Mr. Queed I was ready to try.

Thus the next day I was on a bus to Jefferson High School where I was ushered into the office of the principal,

T. Guy Rogers. When I explained that I wanted to finish high school and needed only a half year more, he stopped me and turned me over to his assistant, Mr. Ivy, to determine if I could be admitted this late into the school term.

Mr. Ivy was most helpful, sympathetic, fully understanding. It was as if he took care of runaways and their problems like mine every day. In the Great Depression my case perhaps was not unusual. In any event, he urged me to start immediately, saying that he would send at once for a transcript of my Bolton High record.

With his help I selected chemistry, English, and a couple of other subjects, including shorthand, which Mr. Queed had urged me to take since it would assist me in taking notes in law school.

Mr. Ivy knew from a phone call to Mr. Queed that I needed to qualify for entrance to the law school sponsored by the San Antonio Public School system. Under Texas law at that time, no undergraduate college work was required before entering a qualified law school — only a high school diploma was.

So, here I was, back in high school! This was where I was supposed to have been last September. And now, provided I didn't fail, I was to graduate with a spring class of seniors, a half school year behind the midterm class I had run away from back in Louisiana.

I would still have to handle the necessary typing for Mr. Queed, as well as my schoolwork — but that night I wrote a long letter home to my folks telling them all about this dramatic development and my plans to enter law school in the fall. I was sure they would be pleased to receive the good news.

I had now been away from home almost six months. At age seventeen, I realized that I was still a long way from growing up, but with the help and encouragement of a number of strangers and friends, I was now back on the right road to growing up as well as defeating my grim opponent. And despite the pitfalls of the Great Depression still ahead, more than ever I felt equal to the challenge, and confident a brighter future beckoned.

AFTERWORD

Yes, I finished Jefferson High School with its spring class of 1933, and then went on to night law school to earn an LL.B. degree and the right to practice law in Texas. There were endless family and economic obstacles in getting that law degree and license, so the expected three-year timetable stretched into four. Altogether, problems caused by the Great Depression and their solutions proved to be a practical school of hard knocks that paralleled and supplemented my formal education.

In the struggle to pay my way through night law school, I changed jobs twice, ending up as office boy in Senator Harry Hertzberg's law firm of Hertzberg and Kercheville. On being sworn in as a lawyer at age twenty-one, I became this firm's youngest member.

My first trip back to my Louisiana home was Christmas 1933, for my father's funeral. By the fall of 1934, I had managed to bring Mother, my two sisters and my terminally ill brother to San Antonio to live with me. Brother Carl remained behind to carve out a life of his own. Dad left many debts, and no assets. Yet Carl personally assumed the burden of paying off all of the debtors just to clear our father's good name, a voluntary action for which I have always admired him.

Sister Oletta partnered with me to house, feed and clothe the family, and pay the burial costs of brother Clyde who passed away within a few months after his arrival in San Antonio.

I met my law school expenses when I unexpectedly fell into an extra part-time job: the State of Texas paid me thirty-five cents an hour to read lessons to a blind classmate, Marcus Roberson.

My friendship with Mr. Queed continued, but contact with Bobby Whittridge, my Stroud cousins, and a number of others mentioned in this story gradually dwindled. Inez Heard and I did indeed date and remained fast friends.

Some of the most exciting chapters of my life happened in my association and friendship with Senator Hertzberg, a most unusual and complicated individual.

Through him I finally met Congressman Maury Maverick socially — quite a different scene from the one when I was a paper boy and yelled headlines so loud he couldn't work!

Senator Hertzberg also introduced me to many other local and nationally prominent politicians, musicians, artists, and circus stars (one in particular who would have thrilled my father was famed cowboy movie and circus star, Tom Mix, who to my surprise was a cultured Rhodes scholar).

In 1937 I chauffeured the Senator on a memorable trip to Chicago and New York City and met more of his contacts in the book, art and circus worlds. This journey took us through Albany, New York, where he bought the collection of circus memorabilia — a miniature circus, Tom Thumb's carriage and numerous other items — that now forms the centerpiece of the Hertzberg Circus Museum in San Antonio.

The Senator died in 1939, but I remained a member of his organization until I joined the army in 1941. My World War II experiences brought about a new direction in my life; however, my legal training remained a valuable, effective tool in my professional career.

I returned to live in San Antonio two more times. The company I worked for, U.S.F. & G., transferred me there in 1956 for five years, and thus I had the pleasure of introducing my "hometown" to my wife and children, renewing old acquaintances, visiting old haunts and recalling my prewar years there. Mr. Queed was now living at the Elks Club, and was delighted to meet my family.

One day I passed a small shop on South Alamo Street which bore the sign "Nano Duran, Electrician." I stopped. It was indeed the same Nano Duran of my carhop days, and we enjoyed a brief reunion. Duran's closed some years after the war, and Nano finally got to do what he had wanted to all along, be an electrician. As I said a final farewell, I thanked him for his helpfulness and kindness when I was a needy teenager in desperate straits.

Thoughts of Nano and of working at Duran's for tips only returned recently as I watched a TV talk program. It featured a person on a one-man crusade to eliminate tipping and replace it with a living wage for employees. "He doesn't stand a chance," I predicted.

Sometime after I quit my job at Duran's I had written

a "Letter to the Editor" of the *San Antonio Express* to blister tipping and substitute decent wages, and the letter was published. A friend, who worked at Duran's four years after me, later told me that he had received a salary plus tips. I couldn't believe my published letter had anything to do with this change of policy, but to find sixty years later that the argument is the topic of a talk show bowled me over.

I'll always remember the kindness of the San Antonio Police who allowed homeless waifs to sleep in their warm basement during the Great Depression. Their headquarters and jail have moved, but the three-story structure still stands, owned and occupied by an attorney.

I hope that some of the flavor of my life, dreams and aspirations, and many of the lessons from my Great Depression experiences, will be of interest, as well as convey some lessons, to young people, and stimulate their elders to remember: life can be hard at times, and at some step along the way of life, all of us need that little boost that I received — a pat on the back, trust, words of encouragement and occasionally even a free meal.

A 1935 photo of Duval Edwards and Inez (Heard) Weatherly taken between the Manhattan Cafe and Majestic Theater in San Antonio.

123

"The Great Depression Taught Us About Poverty."
— Caroline Bird

Appendix

THE GREAT DEPRESSION

It had its beginning on Black Thursday, October 24, 1929, with an historic, gigantic crash on Wall Street, the nickname as well as location of the famous stock market in New York City. The crash was a sudden and deep fall in prices of corporate stocks heard and eventually felt around the world — plunging it on the path to the Great Depression.

That eventful day was followed on Tuesday, October 29, when over sixteen million shares of stock were traded, making it what one famous economist described as "the most devastating day in the history of markets." The final lows for stock values in 1929 were reached November 13, when they were only half as high as in September, but still nearly four times the bottom they would sink to in 1932!

This nose-dive in the value of stocks represented the invested capital that fueled our economy; the crash was the visible evidence of the start of the Great Depression. But just the start, because still three years later stock values had sunk three and four times lower than where they were at the end of that October 1929 day.

It took many years for stocks and the economy to recover from this plunge into the worldwide Great Depression, some effects of which lasted until our entry into World War II.

In fact, the Great Depression left a mark on a vast number of Americans that is just as permanent as memories of World War II are to its veterans. Why would Thomas C. Cochran of the University of Pennsylvania link them in his book *The Great Depression and World War II* (1968, published by Scott, Foresman and Company)?

He may well have expressed the answer in one short statement in his book: "The breakdown of respect for parents and of family sustenance, hope and security undoubtedly had a serious physical and psychological impact on the children of the unemployed who were born and brought up between 1929 and 1940."

And Caroline Bird wrote in 1966 (*The Invisible Scar*) that "... the Great Depression was real, it was awful, and more to the point, it packed a bigger wallop than anything else that happened to America between the Civil War and the Atom Bomb."

As fortunes were lost on Wall Street and elsewhere, many could not bear to watch assets and holdings being wiped out before their eyes, nor face loved ones whose status in life depended on them. They took what was to them the easy way out: personal nose-dives out of tall buildings and off of high bridges, leaving their families to sink or swim — and suffer. Suicides of the prominent and not-so-prominent continued to make headlines day after day.

The total effect of the big crash was not immediate and uniform throughout the land, but spread in ripples from financial centers and headquarters of giant corporations. Like waves on a pond started by a flung rock, the ripples fanned out from the point of origin, gradually touching every village and town and rural area in the forty eight states and on beyond to the rest of the civilized world, and even to a lesser degree to the not-so-civilized areas.

The ripples did not reach Louisiana where I was living, right away. The effect there, as in most places, was a progressive one, of people being laid off in gradually increasing numbers, of small businesses that fed on larger ones closing their doors permanently and throwing more workers into unemployment lines, thus increasing the host of job seekers, of businesses voluntarily going or being forced by creditors into lethal bankruptcies, to end more jobs and initiate more wavelets of unemployment and despair.

One out of every three to four workers (25% to 33-1/3% of employables) in the United States were out of work by 1932 and 1933. In many places this percentage was even higher: *all* able-bodied workers in one entire county in Southern Illinois were virtually unemployed. In some Appalachian mining cities only two or three hundred people out of many thousands were still on the job in 1932! And in Harlan County, Kentucky, there were whole towns with no income at all. People were reported to live on dandelions and blackberries.

These statistics are clearly far worse than those of recessions since World War II, when cries of alarm arise when the national percentage of unemployed creeps up toward 6 or 7 or 8 per cent!

Moreover, those who had jobs often had their salaries and/or commissions reduced in order for the employer to keep from going under. The fortunate ones were mail carriers and certain other lucky government employees on a fixed salary.

Their wages may not have been cut officially, but in some public sectors like public schools, for instance, teachers were paid not with money, but with script — a promise in writing to pay when sufficient tax money arrived in the till. Lack of funds in 1932 and 1933 caused some 2600 elementary schools nationwide to close their doors.

Some grocery stores, banks and other businesses accepted this script as a public service and in hopes of converting it to real money some day. But not all businesses were financially able to do this; for instance, one Colorado bank had its deposits of $650,000 in 1929 reduced to $150,000 by 1933. And times were increasingly hard for these public school teachers, as well as other public servants in the same category.

Three years after that stock market collapse in October 1929, the situation had so deteriorated that the governor of one state closed all banks for twelve days. Not too many weeks later, on February 4, 1933, the Louisiana governor did the same, followed by a growing number of other governors.

Along with increasing business failures was the loss of spirit and hope by more and more individuals, until our nation elected a new president, Franklin D. Roosevelt, in November 1932. He signaled a reversal in that trend of despair when he told the country in his inaugural speech: "The only thing we have to fear is fear itself — ." Thus on March 4, 1933, when he took charge, for the first time optimism and enthusiasm missing for nearly four years was rekindled. And one of his first acts was to declare a nation-wide bank holiday!

The basic cause for this crash and ensuing economic predicament has been argued and debated by experts. And as a consequence of the Great Depression experiences, our government now has in place many devices and schemes calculated to prevent as disastrous a reoccurrence, as well as agencies and procedures to ease the sufferings of individuals should anything that even approaches it occur again. It is my hope, therefore, that there will never be a future time creating a need for another "letter" like this one to be written.

Duval A. Edwards

BIBLIOGRAPHY
(nonfiction only)

The American Writer and the Great Depression. Indianapolis, Bobbs-Merrill, 1966.

BERTON, Pierre: *The Great Depression: 1929-1939*. Canada, McClelland & Stewart, Inc., 1990.

BIRD, Caroline: *The Invisible Scar*. New York, D. McKay Co., 1966.

BONNIFIELD, Paul: *The Dust Bowl: men, dirt and depression*. Albuquerque, U. of NM Press, c1979.

BOARDMAN JR, Fon W: *The thirties: America and the Great Depression*. New York, H. Z. Walck, 1967.

CHANDLER, Lester V: *America's Greatest Depression, 1929-1941*. New York, Harper & Row, 1970.

CHAPEL HILL: *Down and Out in the Great Depression: Letters from the "forgotten man"*. U of NC Press, c1983.

COCHRAN, Thomas C: *The Great Depression and World War II*. Scott Foresman and Co., 1968.

FARRIS, John: *The Dust Bowl*. San Diego, Lucent Books, c1989.

GALBRAITH, John K: *The Great Crash, 1929*. Boston, Houghton Mifflin, 1961, 1972, 1979.

GARRATY, John A: *The Great Depression*. San Diego, Harcourt Brace Jovanovich, c1986.

GOLDSTON, Robert: *The Great Depression: the US in the Thirties*. Indianapolis, Bobbs-Merrill, 1968.

HICKOK: *One Third of a Nation: Lorena Hickok reports on the Great Depression*. Urbana IL, U of Ill Press, c1981.

KATZ, William Loren: *An Album of the Great Depression*. New York, F. Watts, 1978.

KEYLIN, Arleen: *The Depression Years* as reported by the NY Times. New York, Arno Press, 1976.

LACY, Leslie A: *The Soil Soldiers: Civilian Conservation Corps in the Great Depression*. Radnor PA, Chilton, c1976.

McELVAINE, Robert S: *The Great Depression: America, 1929-1941*. New York, Times Book, c1983.

MELTZER, Milton: *Brother, Can You Spare a Dime? The Great Depression, 1929-33*. New York, Knopf, 1969.

MIGNECO, Ronald & Timothy L Biel: *The Crash of 1929*. San Diego, Lucent Books, c1989.

MITCHELL, Broadus: *Depression Decade: from New Era through New Deal 1929-41*. White Plains NY, Sharpe, 1947.

PARADIS, Adrian A: *The Hungry Years: the Story of the Great Depression*. Philadelphia, Chilton, 1967.

ROMASCO, Albert U: *The Poverty of Abundance: Hoover, the Nation, the Depression*. NY, Oxford U Press, 1965.

SHACHTMAN, Tom: *The Day America Crashed*. New York, Putnam, 1979.

SHANNON, David A: *The Great Depression*. Prentice-Hall, 1960.

SOBEL, Robert: *The Great Bull Run: Wall Street in the 1920s*. New York, Norton, 1968.

TAYLOR, Paul: *On the Ground in the Thirties*. Salt Lake City, G. M. Smith, 1983.

TEMIN, Peter: *Did Monetary Forces Cause the Great Depression.* New York, Norton, c1976.

Ten Lost Years: 1929-1939, Memories of Canadians who Survived the Depression. Toronto & Garden City NY, Doubleday, 1973.

TERKEL, Studs: *Hard Times: Oral History of the Great Depression.* Pantheon (Random), 1970.

THOMAS, Gordon & Max Morgan-Witts: *The Day the Bubble Burst, a Social History of the Wall Street Crash of 1929.* Garden City, New York, Doubleday, 1979.

WARE, Susan: *Holding Their Own: American Women in the 1930s.* Boston, Twayne (G.K. Hall), c1982.

WESTIN, Jeane: *Making Do: How Women survived in the '30s.* Chicago, Follett, c1976.

WHISENHUNT, Donald W: *The Depression in the Southwest.* Port Washington, NY, Kennikat Press, c1980.

WORSTER, Donald: *Dust Bowl: southwestern plains in the 1930s.* New York, Oxford U Press, 1979.

ORDER FORM
RED APPLE PUBLISHING

Date _____

Order Number _____

Name _____

Address _____

City, state, zip _____

Telephone _____

I would like to order the following:
The Great Depression and A Teenager's Fight to Survive,
by Duval A. Edwards

$11.95   Quantity _____ Amount _____

Sales tax _____
(Add 7.8% in Washington)

Shipping and handling _____
(1-2 books, add $1.50)
(3-4 books, add 2.00)
(5-6 books, add 2.50)
(7-9 books, add 3.00)
(10+ books, add 3.50)

Total _____

Send payment with order to:
RED APPLE PUBLISHING
PO Box 101
Gig Harbor WA 98335

Telephone: Peggy J. Meyer, (206) 265-6595